# AFRICAN AMERICAN
*Pastoral*
*Care*

# AFRICAN AMERICAN
*Pastoral Care*

*Edward P. Wimberly*

**ABINGDON PRESS**
*Nashville*

AFRICAN AMERICAN PASTORAL CARE

*This book is printed on recycled, acid-free paper.*

**Library of Congress Cataloging-in-Publication Data**

Wimberly, Edward P., 1943–
African American pastoral care/Edward P. Wimberly.
   p.   cm.
Incluces bibliographical references and index.
**ISBN 0-687-00933-2** (alk. paper)
   I. Pastoral theology.   2. Afro-Americans—Religion.   I. Title.
BCV4011.W49   1991
253'.089'96073—dc20ch                                    90-26646

95  96  97  98  99  00  01  02 — 10  9  8  7

MANUFACTURED IN THE UNITED STATES OF AMERICA

# Acknowledgments

Many people have helped to inform the narrative perspective that undergirds this book. Foremost in my mind are my parents, both of whom were storytellers; and students, as well—particularly those in the courses I have taught in Pastoral Psychology and the Black Experience, at Garrett-Evangelical Theological Seminary and at Princeton Theological Seminary— have contributed greatly to the development of this manuscript.

Editorial and typing assistance were provided by Barbara Stinchcomb and Joan Svenningsen, and financial assistance was provided by the Board of Higher Education and Ministry of The United Methodist Church. I also thank seminary president Neal Fisher, Dean Richard Tholin, and my faculty colleagues for their constant support and encouragement.

Without the generous assistance of these many people, it would have been difficult to complete this work. I am eternally grateful to all of them.

*Edward P. Wimberly*

# Contents

# Preface

Since the publication of *Pastoral Care in the Black Church* in 1979, I have become firmly convinced that black pastors approach pastoral care through narrative. It is this insight about such an approach to ministry that motivated me to write this supplement to that book.

A truly narrative style of pastoral care in the black church draws upon personal stories from the pastor's life, stories from the practice of ministry, and stories from the Bible. Genuine pastoral care from a narrative perspective involves the use of stories by pastors in ways that help persons and families to visualize how and where God is at work in their lives and thereby receive healing and wholeness.

This method of pastoral care involves several dangers. The primary danger is that the pastor's own life experience is so subjective and personal that it might be used imperialistically to lead some pastors to think that "my way is the only way." Second, the narrative approach might lead some to think that a personal indigenous style is all that is needed and that formal training has no place. Third, the narrative style might cause the pastor to be less empathetic and thereby transform counselee/parishioner-centered counseling sessions into pastor-focused counseling sessions.

However, a narrative approach need not be imperialistic, unempathetic, or pastor-focused. Storytelling can facilitate growth and empathy, be parishioner-centered, and contribute to the essential qualities of any caring relationship. For example, this approach can enable the pastor to enter the parishioner's world of experience and see things through the parishioner's own eyes. It can help the parishioner take full responsibility for making his or her own decisions. It can enable the parishioner to be specific when describing events. This approach also can help the counselor to openly discuss things that are occurring between the counselor and the parishioner. Finally, it can help the counselor to express his or her feelings about what is taking place in the parishioner's life, in ways that lead to growth.

This book is an attempt to demonstrate that an indigenous approach to caring which relies upon storytelling is one style of pastoral care and counseling that takes place in the black church. Not only is this style already used by pastors, it is a basic method used by black people—lay and clergy—to care for one another. Therefore, this book is written for clergy, seminary students, and lay people who are interested in knowing how they have cared for one another, and how they can improve that care.

# Introduction

Black pastors use many types of stories—long stories, anecdotes, short sayings, metaphors—to respond to the needs of their parishioners. Most specific instances in life situations lend themselves to story formation. For example, stories can be used to address the normal crises people face daily, such as birth, a child's first day at school or at day care; transitions from childhood to adolescence, from adolescence to adulthood; mid-life, old age, and death transitions. Likewise, story formation can occur during periods of crisis: losses such as illness, accidents, changes in residence, and a variety of other events that pose threats to someone's emotional or physical well-being. Stories also can be developed during selective phases of counseling to facilitate the counseling process.

In all these ways, stories function in the caring setting to bring healing and wholeness to the lives of persons and families within the black pastoral-care context. Henry Mitchell and Nicholas Lewter call such stories *soul theology*, the core belief-system that gives shape to the world, that shows how African American people have come to grips with the world in a meaningful way.[1] These core beliefs are embodied in narratives and stories that permeate the church life of African Americans, and black pastors and congregations draw on this narrative reservoir when caring for their members. These narratives suggest ways to motivate people to action, help them to see themselves in a new light, help them recognize new resources, enable them to channel behavior in constructive ways, sustain them in crises, bring healing and reconciliation in relationships, heal the scars of memories, and provide guidance when direction is needed.

Soul theology makes up the faith story that undergirds the stories used by black pastors and parishioners in caring for others. And how that faith story has brought healing and wholeness through storytelling to the lives of African American people is the subject of this book.

## The Faith Story

Mitchell and Lewter point out that core beliefs are expressed spontaneously during crisis situations.[2] Core beliefs are deep metaphors, images that point to the plots or directions of life; they undergird the behaviors of people as they attempt to live their lives, and normally, they are rooted in stories. For the African American Christian, deep metaphors are related to the life, death, and resurrection of Jesus Christ, who liberates the oppressed and cares for the downtrodden. The deep metaphor is informed by the Exodus story and God's involvement with God's people. These deep metaphors and core beliefs are anchored in the story of God's relationship with God's people, as recorded in Scripture and as lived out within African American churches.

The plot that undergirds the deep metaphors of the

Christian story is important to the faith story. Plots tell us why we live on earth; they point to the direction life is taking.[3] Plot in the Christian faith story shows us how our lives are connected to God's unfolding story. The faith story, therefore, answers the question of the "ultimate why" of our existence.

The dominant plot that gives life meaning for the African American Christian is what I call an eschatological plot, one that envisions hope in the midst of suffering and oppression, because God is working out God's purposes in life on behalf of persons. The eschatological plot takes suffering and oppression very seriously without minimizing their influence in life. Yet despite the prevalence of suffering and oppression, God's story of hope and liberation is unfolding. Although the final chapter of the story of liberation awaits consummation at the end of time, during many moments along life's journey, there is evidence of God's presence, bringing healing, wholeness, and liberation.

This eschatological plot which undergirds the faith story of black Christians has been referred to by Mitchell and Lewter as the providence of God:

> The most essential and inclusive of these affirmations of Black core beliefs is called the Providence of God in Western terms. Many Blacks may not have so precise a word for it, and they may not even know that the idea they cling to so naturally is called a doctrine. But in Africa and Afro-America, the most reassured and trusted word about our life here on earth is that God is in charge. This faith guarantees that everyone's life is worth living. The passage that expresses it best is Paul's famous word to the Romans: "And we know that God works in everything for the

good of those who love him and are called according to his plan."[4]

The eschatological plot calls the Christian to faith because each must participate in life and in God's unfolding story, knowing that things will work out in the end. The eschatological plot is important because it does not minimize suffering and oppression, nor does it give suffering and oppression the last word.

A goal of the narrative approach to pastoral care in the black church has been to link persons in need to the unfolding of God's story in the midst of life. The African American pastor has narrated, and continues to narrate, stories that help people catch a glimpse of hope in the midst of suffering. It is by identifying with the story that Christians have linked themselves to purposeful directions in life, despite suffering and pain.

The eschatological plot, through which God is working out healing, wholeness, and liberation on behalf of others, has four major functions: *unfolding, linking, thickening,* and *twisting.*[5] God's plot *unfolds* one scene and one chapter at a time, and one cannot know the end of the story until the entire drama is completed. However, by identifying with faith stories, particularly stories in the Bible, one can learn to participate in God's drama, while trusting God's authorship of the drama and God's plan for the final outcome. In counseling within the black church, this often has meant that the pastor must ensure that the counselee who is identifying with a biblical story reads the whole story before coming to any conclusions. For example, it is important that one continue the story of Joseph and the coat of many colors until Joseph is occupying an important government position for the second time. To stop reading this story before its end may leave the reader feeling that life is tragic. Only at the end of the story can we see God's purposes for Joseph revealed. When one reads the entire story, one can envision hope in the midst of tragedy.

When one identifies with stories that have an eschatological plot in Scripture, one is not only pointed toward God's unfolding story in the midst of life, one is *linked* with the dynamic that undergirds the plot. God's unfolding story is more than a good story with which to identify. It is an ongoing, unfolding story, even today, so when black Christians have identified with that story, they also have linked their lives with the dynamic force behind the events of life. When people are linked to God's unfolding story, their own lives become different. Significant changes take place. People find that life has direction for them, that they have value as human beings. The slaves' identification with Israel's Exodus is illustrative of such positive outcomes. By linking their lives with the unfolding plot of Israel's Exodus, the slaves focused their attention on God, who was also working on their behalf to liberate them.

The eschatological plot also thickens. *Thickening* refers to those events that intrude into God's unfolding story and seek to change the direction of that story for the ill of all involved. The plot often can thicken when suffering stakes its claim on us. This thickening could be the intrusion of oppression and victimization which, for a time, hinder our growth and develop-ment, and it is at such times that we wonder whether God really cares. However, unfortunate negative interruptions are temporary, and the story again begins to unfold in ways that help us to envision God at work, seeking to *twist* the story back to God's original intention, despite the thickening that hindered the plot.

A pastor who understands the working of God through drama can link people with the unfolding of God's story. Such a pastor seeks to help parishioners develop *story language* and *story discernment*, in order to visualize how God's drama is unfolding in their lives. This means that telling and listening to stories become central to the caring process. It also means that people learn to follow the plots of stories, to visualize how God is seeking to engage them in the drama as it impacts their lives.

The eschatological plot, with its emphasis on God's healing presence in life despite suffering and pain, has been the driving force behind the narrative approach of the black church. By telling and listening to stories, black preachers and congregants have sought to help people to envision God's work in the midst of suffering. They have sought to link people with this activity, so that their lives can have significant meaning, despite the reality of suffering.

In addition to the unfolding, linking, thickening, and twisting of plots, faith stories have such therapeutic functions as healing, sustaining, guiding, and reconciling.[6] These are the traditional functions of pastoral care and are very much a part of the narrative approach. However, since a narrative approach to pastoral care cannot determine the impact of a story, one cannot predetermine the impact a story might have on a parishioner or counselee. Nevertheless, stories do impact people's lives in characteristic ways: They can heal or bind up wounds caused by disease, infection, and invasion; they can sustain persons in the face of overwhelming odds and lessen the impact of suffering; they can provide guidance to those who must make decisions, as well as facilitate reconciliation for those who have been alienated from God and others.

Stories are shared by pastors and congregants to call to the attention of people in need how God is at work in their lives—whether God is working through healing, sustaining, guiding, or reconciling. Pastors seek to help people discern where God is working, so that the persons may cooperate with God's unfolding story as it impacts their lives. Once the story is told, the pastor waits for clues from the parishioners and counselees, to discern how God is using the story. Although the storyteller cannot predict how counselees or parishioners will be influenced by the story, the storyteller can use the gift of story for specific purposes—to make points, suggest solutions, decrease opposition to offered care, increase motivation, enlarge understanding of the problem, increase self-recognition, and discover resources.[7] All these purposes serve the primary purpose—to help the parishioners or counselees to envision God's healing and holistic activity working within their lives.

## Pastoral Care, Preaching, and Worship

Storytelling in pastoral care has a different function and context than it does in preaching and worship. In preaching, the purpose is to assist in disclosing the gospel. The context is usually public worship, which uses storytelling to celebrate God's unfolding drama and invites worshipers to participate in that salvation drama. In preaching and in worship, the goals of storytelling are disclosing, inviting, and celebrating in a public context.

Pastoral care, on the other hand, uses storytelling in the context of caring relationships, to help remove the personal and interpersonal obstacles that can hinder people's ability to grow. The goal of pastoral care and counseling, from a narrative perspective, is to use storytelling to strengthen people's personal and interpersonal growth, so that they can respond to God's salvation drama as it unfolds and impacts their lives.

From a narrative perspective, pastoral care can be defined as bringing all the resources of the faith story into the context of caring relationships, to bear upon the lives of people as they face life struggles which are personal, interpersonal, and emotional. The gospel must respond to the personal needs of individuals and families as they face life struggles. This is best done in the private context of pastoral care, rather than in the public context of preaching or worship. Because the context and intent of preaching, worship, and pastoral care are different, the use of storytelling in each ministry is also different.

### Story-listening

So far, this discussion has been devoted to the storytelling aspect of caring. One might conclude that the telling of stories is the main dimension of a narrative approach to pastoral care. The danger of overemphasizing storytelling, however, is that it may ignore the needs of the person facing life struggles. Story-listening is also an important dimension of African American pastoral care, and the narrative approach is a story-listening as well as a storytelling approach.

Story-listening involves empathetically hearing the story of the person involved in life struggles. Being able to communicate that the person in need is cared for and understood is a result of attending to the story of the person as he or she talks. *Empathy* means that we attend to the person with our presence, body posture, and nonverbal responses. It also means using verbal responses to communicate that we have understood and are seeking to understand the person's story as it is unfolding. The care giver also gives attention to and acknowledges the significant feelings of the person as they are expressed in the telling of the story. It is only when the story has been fully expressed and the care giver has attended to it with empathy that the foundation is laid for the utilization of storytelling.

The emphasis must be on story-listening to avoid the trap of shifting the focus from the needs of the person facing life struggles. There are two important ways to prevent this potential abuse of storytelling. First, a growing body of literature on storytelling within the context of counseling and psychotherapy can assist pastors in knowing how to use their own life stories in facilitative ways. Second, pastors need to grow in their own personal life so that their life stories and participation in the faith story will be a reservoir of conflict-free and anxiety-free stories. The ways one can utilize new resources from the counseling litera- ture and can grow so that one's life will be an anxiety-free source of stories will be addressed in later chapters.

## The Limitations of a Narrative Approach

In addition to the danger that a narrative approach might focus on the pastor's needs rather than those of the parishioner or counselee, other limitations to the narrative approach must be addressed as well. First, the storytelling approach is not designed to be the only approach to the problems people face. There are times when direct and confrontational approaches are more appropriate. Sometimes pastors in the priestly role must help people face the truth and assess whether the story the person is living out is healthy or unhealthy. The key is that the pastor must help people judge their own stories in light of the faith story. When there is some discrepancy between the person's own story and the unfolding faith story, this truth should be pointed out by the pastor. Moreover, the pastor should help the counselee to align his or her own life story with God's unfolding story.

Another limitation of the storytelling method is that it may assume that the people in need have Bible knowledge. But what about those who are unchurched or have very few roots in the institutional church? Although the storytelling approach does presuppose some familiarity with biblical stories, many such stories can be used to address the problems people present, if careful thought is given to the reason the stories are being told. One cannot assume that people will find Bible stories objectionable or irrelevant to their needs, simply because of their lack of familiarity. Nor can one assume that there is no religious interest on the part of some counselees. However, this does not give the pastoral counselor license to tell religious stories without prior thought or permission from the counselee. It is always appropriate to ask for permission prior to telling the story. And one need not confine oneself to religious stories. There is rich material in African American folklore from which to draw as well.

## SUMMARY

Black pastors, to care for persons through storytelling:

1. Draw upon their own experiences in life and ministry, as well as upon Bible stories.

2. Utilize storytelling in the context of caring relationships, to foster personal, interpersonal, and emotional growth.
3. Use stories as a means of enriching people's awareness of God's drama unfolding in their lives, despite suffering.
4. Link persons with the unfolding of God's drama in ways that bring healing, sustaining, guidance, and reconciliation.
5. Enable parishioners to develop a language that helps them discern God's work in their lives.
6. Use the resources of the church and the narratives that undergird them to attend to the needs of individuals, families, and small groups. This includes worship and ritual.
7. Use stories in the art of counseling to make points, suggest solutions, facilitate cooperation, increase self-awareness, and discover resources for counseling.
8. Use conflict-free and anxiety-free narratives to help people grow emotionally and interpersonally.

## NOTES

1. Henry Mitchell and Nicholas Lewter, *Soul Theology* (New York: Harper & Row, 1986), p. 11.
2. Ibid., p. 3.
3. James Hillman, *Healing Fiction* (Barrytown, N.Y.: Station Hill, 1983), pp. 9-12.
4. Mitchell and Lewter, *Soul Theology*, p. 14.
5. See James Hopewell, *Congregations, Stories, and Structures* (Philadelphia: Fortress Press, 1987), p. 154.
6. These functions are defined in Edward P. Wimberly, *Pastoral Care in the Black Church* (Nashville: Abingdon Press, 1979), pp. 18-23.
7. See Philip Barker, *Using Metaphors in Psychotherapy* (New York: Brunner & Mazel, 1985), pp. 32-34.

# CHAPTER I

# Pastoral Care and Worship

## Caring and Addiction

The role of the local congregation in pastoral care can best be discerned in the worship life of the black church, but it is not only in corporate worship in the large congregation that pastoral care takes place. Pastoral care in worship also takes place in small groups gathered for Bible reading, exhortation, and prayer and song services to heal physical ills, emotional wounds, and relational hurts. Such services include small groups of people who care about the well being of others.

Although black church worship has been celebrated in literature as emotionally therapeutic for African American Christians, the strength of the worship life has not been only in the Sunday morning service. As in many vital churches, small group meetings called to minister to specific needs of persons and families also have been strong within black churches. In Wednesday night prayer and Bible study meetings, significant hurts have been healed. In the pastor's study, many small groups have prayed for and with people in difficulties. When the choir has surrounded its members in need, significant caring has taken place.

These small group settings are often informal, but ritual is present nonetheless. Here ritual is referred to as repetitive actions which have as their goal the drawing of people into the major story of the faith community. Whenever the goal of ritual draws persons into the major story of the faith community, worship takes place. Moreover, when ritual and worship draw persons into the major story of the faith community, worship and communal resources are brought to bear on personal needs; and when the emotional, interpersonal, and psychological needs of persons are met in the context of ritual and worship, pastoral care takes place.

This chapter looks closely at the role of the laity as caretakers within a ritual and worship context. The emphasis is on defining the role of the laity as caretakers, along with the pastor, in a ritual and worship context. The primary focus is on small groups of from three to forty-five people, called together to perform special rituals of pastoral care for persons in need. Attention also is given to helping the laity define or understand its caring role within the ritual life of the church.

## A Theology of Ministry

In assisting the laity in its role within the caring ministry of the church, it is important to look at the total ministry of the church. Only when the total ministry is understood is it possible to visualize the role of the laity in pastoral care within the ritual and worship context.

Caring within a local black congregation is a response pattern to God's unfolding story in its midst. This unfolding story is one of liberation as well as healing, sustaining, guiding, and reconciling. As a response to God's story, the caring resources of the local black church are used to draw those within the church, as well as those outside the church, into God's unfolding story. By being drawn into God's story, people find resources of care and love to meet their everyday needs. As a response to being drawn into God's story and finding care and love, pastors and laity alike commit themselves to be part of God's ongoing story of liberation and healing. Being committed to God's unfolding story means not only drawing others into that story, but helping others to envision the working of God's story in the midst of their own lives.

Caring is a ministry of the church and cannot be understood apart from the ecclesiology or theology of the church. The mission of the church, from a narrative perspective in the black church, is the continuation of God's story. It is the story of liberation and healing as understood centrally in the book of Exodus, as continued through the life, death, and resurrection of Jesus Christ, and as revealed today within local churches, empowered by the Holy Spirit. The unfolding story of God's rule and reign is characterized by God's ongoing activity to bring all dimensions of the world under God's leadership and story for the purposes of liberation, healing, and wholeness. This results in personal and social transformation.

The purpose of God's rule is to draw all people and nations into God's story. God's story is a story of the defeat of the powers of evil, oppression, and suffering. It is a story of healing and wholeness when people live meaningful lives in community. God seeks to draw people and communities into this story so that the resources of God's reign can be made available to them for their growth and development. Thus, God's rule and reign is about drawing people into God's story so that they might be shaped by the story and begin to see reality the way it is shaped by God's hand and teachings.

The mission of the church in drawing others into the story of God has implications for (1) the church in worship; (2) the church as a caring community; (3) the church in care and nurture; and (4) the church in service.

First, worship is shaped by God's unfolding story. Worship is the act of people in the local church as they gather to celebrate and give praise to God for being drawn into God's story. It is celebration of the fact that they have found meaning and purpose in their lives as a result of being drawn into the story. However, worship is more than an act of celebration and praise; it is a time when the people of God are drawn deeper into the unfolding story of God and are further shaped by this movement. Their vision and character are transformed because of this increased participation in God's story. Their attitudes, behaviors, intentions, and dispositions take on more of the character of God's story. In other words, increased involvement in God's story leads to an increased ability to be concerned about the things that God is concerned about within the church and within the world.

Second, the total life of the local church is shaped in light of God's unfolding story. The local church, as a community, shapes the individual stories of its members into a communal story which reflects the unfolding story of God. This communal story is shaped by the vision that is caught when the community interacts as the people participate in God's unfolding story. As God is revealed in the unfolding drama, the church as a community can glimpse God's intention for it and for the world. The individual stories of all the people are thus shaped by the vision revealed in God's continued action in their midst.

Third, care and nurture result from faithfulness to God's vision revealed within the community. Care given to another because God cares for us draws people into the richness of God's caring resources for healing, sustaining, guiding, and reconciling. Caring is visualizing God's story as it unfolds in church-goers' lives, in spite of the suffering, pain, and crises, and then helping people respond to God's presence and story in their lives. Nurture in the context of care is an awareness of what it means to be a care giver in God's unfolding story within the life of the church. Nurturing takes seriously the importance of understanding persons in need, as well as understanding the best way to respond to them, particularly within a ritual context.

Caring and nurturing are part of the mission of God's church, as that mission unfolds concretely within the church. As such, pastoral care draws people into God's story of healing, sustaining, guiding, and reconciling. It also helps God's people care for others, by helping others to see themselves the way God sees them, to see God at work in their lives, and to know how to respond to God's caring presence. All this takes place in the context of caring relationships.

Finally, community outreach also is a response to being drawn into God's story. While the larger community may not share the same faith story, the church plays a role in assuring that the resources needed for positive mental health and wholeness are available to the community. Sometimes this means that the local church provides the mental health services that are needed. At other times, the church may ensure that a community agency provides the mental health programs needed in the community. In these ways, the local congregation begins to engage in community organization and political activity, working toward the goal of emotional and mental health and wholeness.

## A Case Study of Caring Through Ritual

Over the years, when I have referrals from pastors for counseling services, I make an attempt to keep the pastor informed of the progress of the counseling. When possible and when the need arises, I may also draw the pastor into the counseling to help achieve a certain goal. Of course, this is done with the permission of those in counseling and is based on sound counseling principles. On some occasions, I may also involve carefully chosen relatives or friends from the church to achieve therapeutic ends. This also must be carefully thought out and planned by the pastoral counselor with the counselee.

One such occasion, when I sought not only the participation of the pastor but also the help of key people within the life of the church, concerned the case of a woman whose husband was using cocaine. I present the case here as an example of one means through which both pastors and laity may be involved in pastoral care and counseling.

This case illustrates how ritual and worship can be utilized for therapeutic ends in very small groups of caring persons. The aim is to enable the reader to draw from this case some general insights which pastors can employ to continue the therapeutic function of worship in the black church.

Often pastors, as well as pastoral counselors, are approached about the drug use of family members. This is often very difficult to approach, especially when the user is not open to receiving the help needed. The following case is an example of one model of help, called "intervention." In this model, loved ones and a professional confront the user with the necessity of getting help. The intervention shows the user that the family cares about him or her and, at the same time, indicates that they want something done about the problem.

This case is one in which a couple was referred to me for marital counseling by a pastor who was aware of the husband's drug use. The pastor felt limited in his resources for dealing with the problem and sought my help. As the problem emerged, it became clear to me that the situation was so serious that the husband needed to be hospitalized for the treatment of cocaine addiction. It was at this point that I began to work with the couple toward the goal of hospitalizing the husband.

Initially, the husband described himself as an occasional weekend user and claimed that he had not been using it much lately. At first his wife seemed unconcerned about the problem; later she would realize that she had been what the literature calls a "codependent," a person who contributes to the addiction by making excuses for the addicted persons, bailing them out of trouble, covering for their embarrassing moments, and refusing to confront them with the way their behavior has hurt the codependent. Codependents often find it very difficult to allow their loved ones to undergo the consequences of their actions.

When the husband missed the third session after

calling me that morning to indicate he would be present, I began to realize that something very serious was taking place. He also missed the fourth session, but he attended the fifth session by himself. At that time he disclosed that the problem was more serious and that he was losing control over cocaine. During the following weekend, the wife called me to indicate that she was at her wits' end and that something had to be done. She was ready to try anything because she could not go on the way things were.

At the sixth session, he indicated that he was a serious user of cocaine and that he was freebasing.[1] On some days, his habit cost $400. He had just lost another job and had begun to sell things, including his wedding ring. He knew that life would deteriorate unless he stopped. At age fifty, he saw his life heading for serious ruin.

He found it hard to understand why he did what he did. He wanted to act differently but felt he did not have the power. He remembered the time when he did not smoke, drink, or take drugs, and he began to explore the feeling he had had since childhood that he was oppressed by Satan. He did not believe he was possessed, but he remembered thinking as a child that he had once met Satan face to face. When he had told his mother, she laughed, saying that he must have looked in the mirror. He felt his life was doomed to failure.

A breakthrough came when we were discussing how his wife bailed him out of the trouble. When she had given him money to buy back his wedding ring, he got the ring, but spent some of the money on cocaine. Deeply hurt, his wife indicated to him that she realized she needed to let him go and that she would stop bailing him out of trouble.

He responded quickly by protesting, "You can't leave a person at a time when they are wounded the most. You can't abandon me to this problem." When I asked him if he could explain what he meant, he said that prayer was the only thing that could help him. He talked about a time when a small group of people prayed for his nephew, who had been an alcoholic. Since that prayer, his nephew has been dry and recovering. His wife then informed him that the nephew was part of the 12-step program of Alcoholics Anonymous and had been working with other alcoholics ever since he started to recover. I began to explore with both of them the possibility of arranging a similar kind of small group prayer meeting. He liked this idea, and we began to plan the time when we would come together for a ritual of prayer for his cocaine addiction.

The first thing we planned was the goal for the prayer meeting. We agreed that the focus would be on behalf of the husband to enter a treatment program for cocaine addiction. He didn't want to be in a white treatment program, and I was able to find one administered by African American people. He did want to do something about treatment, but he hoped that prayer would prevent him from having to go into treatment. He felt that his goal was to bind the work of Satan that was controlling the events in his life. I pointed out that although prayer was basic and foundational, he would require a period of recovery in a hospital following our ritual of healing. I indicated that prayer and treatment need to work together. His wife believed in the power of prayer, but she also knew that prayer would be the beginning of his treatment, rather than the end. He agreed to begin with the ritual of prayer and then wait to see what would happen.

Once we agreed on this goal, we discussed a possible date and the persons who would be part of this small group to pray for healing and deliverance. We decided that the pastor, the pastor's wife, the couple's goddaughter, and a recovering cocaine addict would be there with us. I left it to the couple to call the people and make the arrangements.

Finally the day arrived. When all were present, the pastor began to explore the problem with the husband. They talked back and forth, and the pastor quoted several Bible verses which focused on the availability of God's grace for times such as this. The pastor knew enough about the husband to use verses that made him think. One of the husband's major concerns was his status in life—that all his friends seemed to be making something of their lives. The pastor knew that the husband focused his life in the wrong direction for success and that his problem had spiritual roots. The pastor also shared his struggle with his own son, who had been hooked on drugs, and he seemed to have great empathy for the husband's predicament, although he knew the man needed to go into treatment for help. The husband seemed to feel cared for by the pastor.

Others offered words of encouragement, and some quoted helpful Bible verses. When the pastor asked me what I thought, I said I had listened with great joy to their dialog, when the husband had indicated that he knew the treatment program was necessary. I had waited for the husband to indicate that himself, and I pointed out that his ultimate recovery was his embracing of the purpose he knew God had created him to fulfill. He had known for some time that his ministry would be to help others like himself. In fact, he had begun to attend school for that purpose when he first encountered cocaine. The group acknowledged that everyone knew there was a special purpose for which he was called, and all felt he had to embrace this purpose as part of his healing.

Then as we stood in a circle holding hands, the pastor asked me to begin the prayer and said that others could follow. I began by thanking God for all God's servants who were concerned enough about their loved one to join in prayer for his healing and deliverance. I indicated the reason we were here, asking God to visit us in a very special way with his power and Spirit. At that point, the focus was on the husband and his feeling about being oppressed by Satan. I asked God to come against the evil that was befalling the husband, and as I prayed, the others responded, "In the name of Jesus." I asked that the work of Satan be bound in the name of Jesus and that the husband be empowered with the Holy Spirit to fight the difficult battle ahead. The members of this special prayer group responded, "In the name of Jesus."

After I finished, others began to pray. Concern was raised for the wife and the difficulties she has encountered. Others prayed that the husband would do what he needed to do. The godchild prayed for their future relationship and indicated how much that relationship meant to her.

When the pastor prayed, he seemed to be in direct touch with the husband's thoughts. He addressed all his arguments about not going into treatment; he addressed the needs he would have over the next few weeks in treatment. Then he prayed for the binding of Satan's work and quoted Scripture. When he prayed for the husband, he touched his head and his stomach, as if to find the bodily source of the problem. Then he read Ephesians 3:14-21, emphasizing the prayer that God strengthen the husband in the inner man, so that Christ would take up permanent residence in his heart.

Following this reading, the wife collapsed. The frustration of all the years of pain seemed to have left her weak. Her husband and the whole group began to minister to her. They prayed with her and began to hum in low voices until she felt better.

Two days after the prayer meeting, the wife told me that her husband had entered treatment. She expressed her appreciation and we talked about the spouse program that she needed to take part in at the hospital. I indicated my desire to follow through with counseling once the program had ceased.

### A Narrative Reflection

Worship was a vehicle used in pastoral care to help draw the husband into God's unfolding purposes for his life. The worship service included sharing, music, Bible quoting, and praying. The aim of that worship service was to enable the husband to see that people loved and cared for him and that God was in the midst of his life, seeking to bring wholeness to it.

In the ritual of worship, he acknowledged an awareness of God's presence and work in his life. He knew that God had a purpose for him, but he was slow to allow himself to embrace God's vision and story in his life. Those who cared for him asked God to give him the power to enter the treatment program because they knew that on the other side of treatment, there was a new story for his life.

Worship also challenged the values that were the center of his life. He had a hard time letting go of his images of success, but worship introduced him to the fact that the story he was embracing would lead him into further destruction. Therefore, worship sought to draw him out of the old story that was leading him to destruction and take him into a new story that would lead to hope and fulfillment.

Worship was also a vehicle of God's grace for the couple. The Scriptures that were shared assured the husband that he was loved and that he was a child of God. Ephesians 3:14-21 summarized our meeting together and helped to summarize our intent, which was to strengthen him inwardly so that he could fully engage in the recovery process. By sharing experiences from his own life and disclosing that his own son had been crippled by drug addiction, the pastor showed his care, letting the husband know that his own scenario was the same as that of others before him and that those who loved him would not give up on him.

The most crucial dimension of the worship service was the sharing of the witness of God at work in the husband's life by those who loved the couple. He could not see it, nor could he believe that God had any interest in our prayers for him. It was important for those who cared to witness what they saw God doing, and it was this sharing and witnessing that laid the foundation for reassessing his own life story.

In summary, the small group prayer meeting was designed (1) to share with the husband God's love and grace; (2) to share with him in ways that would draw him further into God's unfolding story; (3) to give him encouragement to enter treatment; and (4) to enable him to discern his role in God's salvation drama.

## The Role of the Pastor

The role of the pastor in Caring and Addiction is to create an environment of concern and care; to enable the worshipers to pray and sing, keeping the needs of people in mind; and to use Scripture and exhortation to encourage those in crisis to have the courage and strength to meet the emotional and interpersonal tasks.

The use of worship to address the early concerns of addiction is very appropriate. In the husband's case, the roots of his addiction were the feelings of being unloved and not cared for by others or by God. He used drugs and alcohol to try to stamp out the feelings of worthlessness and unlovability, but the more he tried to get away from those feelings, the more he went into bondage to his addiction. Worship and the presence of caring others spoke directly to his feelings of being unloved and worthless, and provided the basis for meeting his core needs. The pastor's role helped to facilitate the mediation of grace through worship and caring relationships.

### NOTES

1. Freebasing, converting cocaine into a smokable form sometimes known as crack, is one of the purest forms of using cocaine and is very addictive. Smoking cocaine enables the drug to reach the brain in eight to ten seconds. The high is short-lived, lasting only two to five minutes. The crash is intense and happens abruptly. Freebasing stimulates craving, and many addicts go on binges known as a "run," which can cost as much as $1,000 a day, leaving the addict in a total state of confusion. Psychiatric symptoms include paranoia, severe depression, and emotional volatility. Other risks include brain seizure, respiratory failure, and heart attack. See Arnold M. Washton, *Cocaine Addiction: Treatment, Recovery and Relapse Prevention* (New York: W. W. Norton & Co., 1989), pp. 14-16.

# CHAPTER II

# Pastoral Care and Support Systems

## Illness and Bereavement

The crisis of loss creates a cessation and interruption of important interacting patterns and sustained relationships which have been taken for granted. It is also a rupture in the existing narrative of life, because the experience of loss is the disruption of a narrative. The death of a loved one causes a revising of the story one has been living. For some, a death means fashioning a completely new story for one's life. The crisis is personal and individual, and so is the story about it.

This chapter illustrates how a pastor from the continent of Africa brought the resources of the church to bear upon a family facing the illness and loss of a loved one. The focus is on how the black church, as a support system, sustained the bereaved family by bringing the unfolding story of God to bear upon its needs.

### The Nature of Bereavement

Bereavement is the sudden cessation of a close and abiding relationship.[1] Bereavement often elicits negative emotions called grief, or mourning, which come after the death of a person who has had a particular place in one's life. This follows a somewhat characteristic pattern as the bereft try to fill a void made in their lives by this loss.

The basic tasks for the bereaved person are to achieve emancipation from bondage to the deceased, readjust to a world in which the deceased is missing, and form new relationships.[2] Another task is to revise and edit one's life story without the deceased. These tasks are difficult because the impact of the death of a loved one is apt to stun bereaved persons to the point of immobilization and disorganization.

Those who suffer grief sometimes want to avoid the pain associated with the grief experience. After many attempts on the part of the bereaved to avoid that pain, the grieving process itself must be accepted if adequate mourning is to take place. According to Erich Lindemann, once the grief process is accepted, the bereft begin to deal with the memory of the deceased person, and this, in turn, is followed by relief in tension. Moreover, Lindemann discovered that if others care for the bereaved for four to six weeks, that is an appropriate length of time to help them reach an uncomplicated and undistorted grief reaction.[3]

Certain characteristic symptoms appear in persons suffering bereavement. Lindemann enumerates the following five components of the grief syndrome: (1) body distress; (2) guilt; (3) hostile reactions; (4) loss of patterns of conduct.[4] As a result of the impact of loss, the bereaved suffer tightness in the throat, shortness of breath, the need to sigh, empty feelings in the stomach, and lack of muscular power. The senses are altered to the degree that there may be a sense of unreality and a feeling of increased emotional distance from others.

Often guilt and hostile anger are evidenced when the bereaved accuse themselves of negligence and look for evidence to corroborate this allegation. Moreover, anger may be exhibited toward relatives and friends of the deceased, through a loss of warmth in relationships and a feeling of abandonment on the part of the bereaved.

Patterns of interaction are disrupted by the death of a loved one, resulting in a restlessness, an inability to remain in one place, an aimless moving, a continued search for something to do. There is also a lack of any capacity to initiate and maintain patterns of activity, for the grief sufferer discovers that many of the activities that were done with the deceased or in relationship to the deceased have lost their meaning.

There may be preoccupation with the image and memory of the deceased, often an attempt to deny the death and recover the presence of the lost loved one.[5] There is a yearning or seeking for the loved one, an attempt to achieve reunion with the deceased.[6]

Normal grieving is characterized by three phases. First, the grief sufferers yearn for the lost loved ones and experience anger toward the loved ones for abandoning them. The second phase begins when the bereaved accept the fact that neither yearning nor anger will bring the loved ones back. This leads to despair and disorganization in the lives of the bereaved. Following this phase is a period of reorganization, in which the bereaved turn toward the world and begin to find new relationships and meaning in life. During this period, the grief sufferers either begin the task of revising and editing the old story or begin to develop a new story without the deceased.

During the process of grief work, it is important for the bereaved to experience and express their yearning for and anger toward the deceased. In this way they can give up the deceased and accept the fact that the deceased is gone forever. Only then can they accept the reality that loved ones are separate from themselves and can be lost. Failure to consciously experience and express the yearning for and anger toward the deceased leads to an arresting of the grief process, which eventuates in inappropriate attempts to carry out a reunion with the deceased and, ultimately, to pathological mourning.[7]

## Bereavement Ministry: A Case Example from a Black African Pastor in a Black Church

This is a report of an African pastor who ministered to a dying parishioner and the parishioner's family before and after his death. The focus of the pastor's concern was a black male in his late fifties who was dying from cancer. Prior to the discovery of the malignancy, the parishioner had sustained injuries in a serious car accident, and initially, the illness was linked to complications associated with that accident. However, during the period of convalescence it was discovered that he was terminally ill with cancer of the liver. When told of his disease, the parishioner did not accept the prognosis, refusing to admit he was dying. Rather, he insisted that a good job was waiting for him and that he would return to work.

The parishioner's immediate family consisted of a second wife and a son from his first marriage. The second wife did not live with the husband at the time of his illness; the father and son were estranged and had not seen each other for many years.

The parishioner's extended family consisted of two younger sisters who lived in the area and an older sister living in the Deep South. The two younger sisters had a good relationship with their brother, were upset about his illness, and were concerned about his inability to accept the fact that he was dying. The older sister, however, had a much closer relationship with her brother, probably because she had taken care of him during his childhood.

The man's relationship with the pastor was a comfortable one. The pastor had visited the parishioner periodically in the hospital since the accident. The pastor was concerned about the dying man's inability to accept his impending death, and he expressed this concern to the two younger sisters. While talking with the sisters, the pastor discovered that the dying man probably would be much more willing to talk about his problems with his older sister. Therefore, the pastor sent for this sister, and she came as a result of the pastor's initiative. The pastor found that the dying parishioner was able to express his fears to his older sister and finally was able to accept the fact that he was dying. The pastor also contacted the man's son and informed him of his father's condition. As a result of this effort, the son and father were able to establish some form of reconciliation before the father died.

Following the death of the parishioner, the pastor turned his concern to the bereaved family. He discovered that the second wife, the three sisters, and the son had become a fellowship group for one another. The pastor helped to strengthen this support system by using the wake and the preparation of the funeral service to facilitate the grief process among the members of the fellowship group. He found that their participation in preparing the funeral service stimulated them to express their feelings concerning the beloved brother, husband, and father.

This African pastor had trained many lay people in his congregation for times of bereavement. After discovering that many of the parishioners were from the South and the West Indies, and seemed to automatically know what to do in terms of the crisis of loss, he exploited many of those natural leanings and involved these persons in discussion groups surrounding such crises. When there was a need for these persons' services within the congregation, he would call on them to assist others.

The pastor trained these lay people to share stories from their own lives, to encourage the bereaved to share their stories of hurt and pain. He informed them that a brief story from the lives of the care givers could assist the bereaved to review their own relationships with the deceased and enable feelings of bereavement to be expressed. The pastor warned them, however, to tell their stories in ways that kept the bereaved's needs for grieving central.

According to the African pastor, much of his knowledge concerning bereavement ministry was a result of his African heritage. Death was accepted as a fact of life in his community in Africa, and many extended family obligations were associated with the death of a loved one and the bereavement process.[8] As "eldest son," the pastor's obligation to the family during the bereavement period had consisted of assisting with funeral arrangements and carrying out the father's wishes concerning the remaining family. His participation in a consultation group and a seminar on death, dying, and bereavement were also very helpful in shaping his bereavement ministry.

## A Narrative Reflection on the Case

*The Black Pastor as Diagnostician*

In the case just described, the pastor became aware that the parishioner refused to accept the fact that he was dying of cancer. This refusal to accept a given reality is called denial. Following the diagnosis, the pastor actively sought to ascertain what sources existed within the family to assist the dying patient through his difficulty and to help him face the reality of death.

The pastor became cognizant of several family resources. The patient's second wife revealed a concern about him and attempted to lend support. In addition, the pastor discovered three sisters, who emerged as the most significant sources of support for the dying patient. An adult son, whose communication with the father had been nonexistent for a period of time, also was considered a potential avenue of support.

Aside from family resources, the pastor assessed resources within the church for support of the dying parishioner. Some members had been trained to be of assistance, and religious ceremonials would provide support. The pastor also became aware that traditions among the members, particularly those from the South and West Indies, provided a set of customs which defined the responsibility of church members and friends to persons in crisis. Thus a framework existed with which to support the parishioner and ease him in his dying moments. Through the support of the family, the social network, the church and its heritage, and the values of the black subculture which defined the behavior of persons toward others in crises, the pastor recognized the existence of a variety of resources available before and during death, as well as throughout the subsequent bereavement of the family.

Of great help to the black African pastor were the influential cultural patterns in Africa which informed his sensitivity to the role of extended families in ministering to the dying. He utilized knowledge from his past, and the sensitivities toward the role of support systems acquired from his background, in his bereavement ministry to the congregation.

The key to the use of the cultural patterns of the extended family, the support system, and the funeral, was the fact that these patterns were embodied in the central narrative of the faith tradition. Those in the extended family were part of God's unfolding story; those in the caring support system of the church were part of God's unfolding story. When these people shared stories of bereavement from their own lives, they included testimonies of God's presence in the midst of death. Moreover, the support system shared a common faith story, which, when shared, held out hope in the midst of tragedy.

The wake and funeral were vehicles for assisting the family through the grieving process. As part of caring, the pastor purposely employed the funeral and the wake to help the bereaved discern God's presence in the midst of their grief. Through the funeral and wake, they could encounter the spacious resources of God's story of grace and hope.

The funeral also laid the groundwork for enabling the bereaved to revise and edit their stories. Images of God's presence in the lives of those who were bereaved in Scripture held out hope for developing new life scenarios. The liturgy of the funeral gave the message that God will assist you in fashioning a new story without the presence of the deceased.

The parishioner in this case had been largely uncommunicative about his condition, with the pastor as well as with two of his sisters. However, after learning of another sister, with whom the brother would be willing to talk, the pastor facilitated the arrival of the third sister, which resulted in the dying patient's discussion of his fears and his acceptance of the fact that he was dying. Moreover, after the pastor brought the dying man and his sister together, they began to share stories of their lives together when they were young. These memories and stories helped to shore up his courage so that he could face the task of dying; they secured the bonds between the dying man and his sister. He was sustained and nurtured by sweet memories and died knowing that his life was worthwhile and that he was loved.

Essential to the narrative understanding of caring ministry to the bereaved is the envisioning of the funeral and the caring as being linked to God's unfolding drama in our lives. God's unfolding story is a drama made up of episodes, scenes, chapters, and a plot. The funeral and the ministry of caring in God's name are miniplots in the midst of God's unfolding macro-plot. The macro-plot of God involves death and rebirth made possible by Jesus Christ. The salvation drama is made up of dying with Christ and rising with Christ. Therefore, in ministry to the dying and the bereaved, the task is to draw the people into God's salvation drama of death and rebirth.

Reunion of the loved ones with a dying patient is one illustration of how renewal and rebirth are possible despite the imminence of death. In the described case, the resources of God's ongoing story of salvation undergirded and enabled the rebirth of new relationships. The act of being drawn into God's salvation drama offered new possibilities and hope, in spite of pain and suffering.

As the bereft are drawn into the salvation drama, the foundation is also being laid for them to begin to revise and edit a different narrative, one that is without the loved one. By being linked with God's unfolding drama of death and rebirth, the bereft find courage to begin a new life and a new narrative without the deceased. A new narrative is begun with hope and expectation, knowing that God is in the revising process.

## The Pastor as Mobilizer of Support Systems

The African heritage of the caring pastor in this case made him sensitive to the role of support systems in life transitions. His cultural heritage had built into it traditions of community support and ceremonial practices to aid those in life transitions. These supports and practices gave him a special sensitivity toward knowing how to utilize support systems in bereavement situations with families outside his cultural background.

The major role of the African pastor in the crises of dying and bereavement was to bring the resources of the support system to bear upon the emotional and interpersonal needs of the dying patient and the grieving relatives. By accomplishing this, the pastor (1) provided opportunities for relatives and friends to identify and empathize with one another; (2) provided opportunities to share in a common story of the faith tradition; (3) provided a ritual and worship context for linking and connecting with a meaningful religious plot which brought renewal and rebirth in the midst of suffering; (4) provided a loving and caring group of lay persons and family who facilitated the expression of feelings of grief and mourning; and (5) encouraged the lay care givers to help the grief sufferers use stories from their own lives as a means of facilitating the grief process.

In order to assist the support system in the case of bereavement and dying, the pastor helped the bereaved and the dying parishioner to maintain significant ties with others, which helped them to sustain their emotional and spiritual well-being in the face of death. The support system helped the dying man and his family satisfy their needs for love, affection, and continued participation in meaningful relationships in the midst of suffering.

The use of a support system enabled the pastoral care to be the best within the African and African American church context. The support system helped to sustain the dying man during his last days on earth. It brought healing through the renewal of relationships, helped to guide the grief sufferers through the grief process, and enabled the bereaved and the dying man to be linked with the ongoing drama of God's salvation.

## NOTES

1. This definition is contained in Erich Lindemann, "Symptomatology and Management of Acute Grief," *Crisis Intervention,* ed. Howard J. Parad (New York: Family Service Association, 1976), p. 7.

2. See Lindemann, "Symptomatology of Acute Grief," pp. 7-21, for his reference to basic tasks for the bereaved.

3. Ibid.

4. Ibid.

5. John Bowlby, "Pathological Mourning and Childhood Mourning," *Journal of the American Psychoanalytic Association* 11 (July 1963): 501.

6. Murray C. Parkes, "Seeking and Finding a Lost Object: Evidence from Recent Studies of the Reaction to Bereavement," *Social Science and Medicine* 4 (1970): 187-201.

7. Bowlby, "Pathological Mourning," p. 505.

8. For readings in African pastoral care and counseling, see Abraham Adu Berinyuu, *Towards Theory and Practice of Pastoral Counseling in Africa* (Frankfurt: Peter Lang, 1989), pp. 82-98; *Pastoral Care to the Sick in Africa* (Frankfurt: Peter Lang, 1988); Masamba ma Mpolo, "African Pastoral Care Movement," and "African Traditional Religion, Personal Care In," *Dictionary of Pastoral Care and Counseling* (Nashville: Abingdon Press, 1990), pp. 11-12, 12-13.

# CHAPTER III

# Pastoral Care
# and Life Crises

## Birth, Adolescence, Young Adulthood, Middle Adulthood, Older Adulthood

Members of the church community who are facing predictable life transitions often call on black pastors and lay people. These transitions which occur throughout the life cycle sometimes are referred to as developmental crises. These crises usually are growth opportunities, and while they may present some difficulties for those who face them, pastors and caring lay people can respond with empathy and compassion in ways that help those in crisis to grow.

The focus in this chapter is on ways the black pastor and caring lay people can respond to these predictable transitions through the use of a narrative approach. Black pastors, as well as the laity, can draw upon a rich story resource from their own lives and from Scripture, which they can bring to bear upon the lives of persons facing these life transitions.

### Life Transitions

Life transitions, as crises, are periods when individuals face obstacles brought on by normal changes from within the person, obstacles which cannot be resolved by the customary ways of resolving crises.[1] Factors that contribute to the onset of these developmental crises include the birth of a child, a child entering school for the first time, the onset of adolescence, a young adult leaving home, marriage, and the onset of middle and old age. These times are characterized by brief periods of increased tension, periods of risk when customary ways of resolving problems do not work, the seeking of help from significant others to resolve the crisis, and the trying of new ways to come to grips with the new challenge. Successfully coming to grips with the life crisis involves (1) facing the problem head on; (2) working on the various emotional and social tasks presented by the problem; (3) coming to some understanding of what one is experiencing; and (4) talking with caring others about the situation.

Each life transition has its own dynamics and patterns. Black pastors and laity can benefit from understanding some predictable crises and the tasks people must accomplish when facing these crises.

## Birth as a Life Crisis

Pregnancy is a crisis for the pregnant mother as well as for those whose lives are impacted by the pregnancy, which disrupts the ordinary ways the mother thinks, feels, and relates. Emotional upsets, role changes, and communication problems must be worked through.

The changes that take place within the expectant mother are normal, but they can cause tension with significant others. Metabolic changes cause the expectant mother to experience mood swings. Concerns that may arise between the expectant mother and her own mother may cause tension. The expectant mother's preoccupation with the pregnancy can cause the expectant father to feel left out. Any unresolved issues the mother has with sexuality also may surface and cause tension. New roles, as well as adjustments to new circumstances, are required of all involved. Sometimes unresolved marital issues may surface during pregnancy as well.

These examples of changes brought on by pregnancy show that it is a predicable and normal life crisis. It requires the expectant mother and significant others to make changes in their lives and attitudes. And it is significant that pregnancy provides an opportunity for the pastor and caring persons to respond with empathy and care.

The church takes a significant role when the pastor and caring members enable it to use its natural faith tradition in helping the expectant mother and significant others to be drawn into the unfolding story of God. For churches that baptize infants, baptism is an important means of drawing the entire family into God's ongoing story. For churches that dedicate infants, with emphasis on believer's baptism, this also is a way to draw the child and the family into God's drama unfolding in the midst of the church. Preparation for baptism or dedication prior to the birth can help the expectant family discern the upcoming event as part of God's unfolding drama.

The role of the pastor and caring lay people is to help those involved (1) understand what is taking place as a result of the pregnancy; (2) facilitate the expression and acceptance of the feelings of those whose lives are directly impacted; and (3) help those involved to mobilize resources for responding positively to the crisis. Stories can be used at any of these points to assist in the resolution of the crisis. This is illustrated well by the following case illustration of a pastor who responds to a husband whose wife is pregnant for the first time.

Jane was in the fifth month of pregnancy, the second trimester. James went to the pastor very perplexed because he could not predict his wife's moods, and he resented the fact that she refused sexual relationships with him more often since she had been pregnant. He complained that she was always sick and wanted him to wait on her, that the house never looked right, and that she always seemed tired.

The pastor discovered in their conversation that James had no understanding about the nature of pregnancy or about what pregnant women normally experience. He was not aware that pregnancy brought on mood swings and new psychological and emotional tasks for the expectant mother. He had no knowledge of how to be supportive of his wife. James was facing a crisis and needed the help of his pastor. The pastor knew that James needed to understand pregnancy as a life crisis. James also needed to know that his wife's reactions were a normal part of bringing a new life into the world and that his role as a supportive and empathic mate was essential for Jane to feel secure in her pregnancy.

The pastor spent time listening to James and allowed him to express his feelings of resentment and confusion without censoring those feelings. He wanted James to be comfortable and to look on the pastor as a friend. The pastor felt this was an essential foundation for the time when he would help James understand his wife's needs and how he could respond to them.

The pastor decided to relate a scenario from his own

experience as a husband who had faced the crisis of birth for the first time. His goals for relating the story were to foster increased empathy, help James identify with the pastor's plight as a way to understand his own plight, and to enable James to identify with the solution the pastor had brought to the crisis. The pastor hoped that through the scenario James would come to understand his wife's needs better and be able to respond supportively.

The pastor told James that as a young man, he never had been around a pregnant woman. His father never mentioned anything about the nature of pregnancy or about how a male should respond; his peers were not available, since he had cut himself off from them when he had married. Rather, the pastor had to learn the hard way, by discovering things on his own through reading. In fact, he had no resources other than what he read. The pastor told James that he was quite surprised to learn that what his wife was experiencing was normal. Once he understood what was happening, he was able to be more caring toward his wife. He felt that when he did not know about natural mood swings, he had been resentful, but the resentment disappeared when he understood the nature of pregnancy.

After James heard the pastor's story, he was able to see clearly his wife's needs and that he needed to be supportive. The pastor's skillful use of his own life experience enabled James to understand his own crisis. It helped him to visualize the different role he needed to play, to clear up negative perceptions, and to work through negative feelings.

## Adolescence as a Life Crisis

Adolescence is a shaky bridge between childhood and adulthood, a predicable life crisis brought on by physiological changes. The major task of adolescents is to correlate the way they see themselves as persons with the way others see them. During this period of identity formation, both boys and girls begin to negotiate who they are, apart from others, as well as in relationship to others. It is a time of finding one's own place in the world and developing the kinds of skills needed for social and economic well-being. Some problems for black youths are a result of traditional racial climate and the reliability of family and extended family support.

One of the major tasks of adolescence is learning to negotiate the strong impulses that are welling up inside. The task involves developing a mature sexual identity and controlling one's sexual impulses in healthy and constructive ways. The major difficulty that faces contemporary adolescents is the absence of a language of sexuality for youth that conveys strong relational values and encourages the postponing of sexual expression. Relational values refer to learning the value of friendship and the worth of persons of the opposite sex as objects of love and respect, rather than as objects for sexual gratification. Pastoral care from the perspective of relational values helps youths put sex in the context of marriage, as an expression of love, respect, and responsibility.

The narrative approach lends itself well to helping youths develop a language of sexuality. Narrative, by its very nature, encourages relationships. The best way to teach the language of sexuality is for parents to share with their children the struggles they underwent as youths.

I once conducted an intergenerational worship service for youths and their parents. I encouraged the parents to share with their children what it was like for them as teenagers. I asked them to tell of the conflict that existed between them and their parents, what the peer morality was like at that time, the fears they had in dating, and the courting strategies they used.

One grandmother about seventy-five years of age told that when she was reared in Alabama in the early 1890s, kids did not have the kind of freedom they have today. She had several brothers and sisters, and her parents wanted to know her whereabouts at all times, though the boys had a little more freedom than the girls. She also described the rules for dating: Boys could visit her only when one of her parents was home. There were dances, but her parents had to know who was sponsoring the dance before they would allow her to go. If her parents did not have confidence in the person or group holding the dance, she was not permitted to attend. She said that she had felt her parents were too strict, and she could hardly wait until she was an adult so that she could be free of her parents' domination.

The pastoral care goals of this exercise were to (1) foster better relationships between the generations; (2) lay a positive foundation for open relationships between parents; (3) help youths feel they were understood by their parents; and (4) create a language of sexuality that includes more than sexual intercourse. Narrative sharing helped to do this. That is, by relating and sharing stories about their lives as teenagers, the parents helped the youths to envision the true tasks of adolescent growth. Moreover, the youths realized that sexual intercourse is not the answer to the complex growth issues involved in establishing identity. Black men, and fathers, in particular, need to be part of this kind of narrative sharing so that black males can learn that an adolescent's identity needs are more complex than the making of babies.

Pastoral care with adolescents is intergenerational. Black youth today has turned to its peers as though peers are the family. This is an important dimension of gang activity in urban areas, and the fostering of better relationships between parents and youths through narrative pastoral care can provide an alternative. Pastoral care from an intergenerational perspective can help the youths feel that they are part of the family and do not need to depend totally on the peer group for support. Although the peer group is essential for the accomplishment of some of the tasks, positive relationships between a youth and his or her parents assist greatly in establishing adolescent identity.

## Young Adulthood as a Life Crisis

Young adulthood marks the onset of maturity—physically, psychologically, and socially. The young adult's physical maturation is complete. His or her identity as a separate, yet significantly related person, has a firm foundation; the person has had a chance to develop basic skills of communicating and getting along with others.

The major tasks of young adulthood include making important choices. First, young adults must develop skills for surviving economically. Second, they must decide whether to remain single or marry, and whether to establish a family. Third, they must decide what role religion will play in their lives. Finally, they must find their own way in the world and make their contributions to the world.

Increasingly, the pastoral care concerns of black

young adults are intergenerational family concerns. It does appear that the launching of black young adults into full participation in society requires positive contact with and support from the older generation. For socioeconomic and emotional reasons, many African American and Caucasian young adults are postponing entrance into full participation in the major tasks of young adulthood. I have heard many comments by parents of young adults between the ages of eighteen and thirty, wondering when their children will finally leave home and establish their own lives. Although it is an expectation of American culture that young adults leave home and begin to make their own way in society, these expectations are being altered by the reality of what some are now calling the "postponed generation." Many young adults feel ill-equipped emotionally to face the world. Many feel they do not yet have all the resources from the parental home needed to negotiate in the world.

Pastoral care from a narrative perspective involves the creation of a context in which young adults and their parents can share stories concerning the postponing of the launch into adulthood. The generations seem to have difficulty communicating because the postponed launch is a new phenomenon that has emerged in the last fifteen years. Creating an atmosphere where stories are shared can help bridge the gap between the generations.

One reason for the postponed generation is that children born after 1960 feel less parented than those of previous generations. Within the African American community, the foundations of the black extended family are crumbling, single-parent families are on the increase, and even in a two-parent home, both must work if the family is to survive economically.

These factors contribute to the feelings of not being adequately parented. Too, many young adults feel that they were abandoned by their parents and given to others, particularly the school, to raise. Pastoral care for these young adults must take narrative seriously.

The specific tasks for narrative pastoral care with young adults include establishing an atmosphere in which where parents and young adults feel free to share their stories, enabling the young adult to share what it is like to face the outside world; enabling the parents to share stories of their own launching and the kinds of support they had; and allowing the pastor to share his or her own stories of launching. The ultimate goal for this intergenerational narrative approach is to provide the necessary bonding between the generations and the adequate parenting that has been lacking. Bonding between generations can provide the emotional support needed by young adults to enable them to remain emotionally whole as they negotiate in the world. Narrative sharing is the most natural means of bonding at this stage, since it enables the young adult to remain a mature person who is leaving home. The following example illustrates how to create a context of narrative sharing across generations.

A mother whose newly married son lived at home because of financial reasons sought the pastor's help. Both parents had had reservations, but had reluctantly agreed to participate in this new arrangement after their son convinced them that the problems would be minimal. However, they had made no effort to talk about how to handle conflict, nor had they discussed how a new arrangement with a daughter-in-law in the home might effect them. The mother felt that she had put forth her best effort, but had become a prisoner in her own home. She wanted out of the arrangement.

The pastor listened and empathized with the mother. He shared with her the similar problem his own parents had with his younger brother. The pastor was realistic with the mother about the nature of the problem. Such an arrangement, he felt, should be only temporary because there was so much conflict.

When the mother asked the pastor how she could address the problem, he suggested that she be frank with her son and daughter-in-law. When the pastor asked how her husband felt about this, she said that he shared her feelings. She then asked the pastor if he could be with her and her husband as they spoke with their son and his wife. The pastor agreed, explaining that his role would be to help all of them share their feelings and attempt to solve the problem as they explored alternatives.

Intergenerational support through narrative sharing is essential in order for the young adult to accomplish the tasks of being a young adult. I have illustrated how a narrative approach can address the concern of leaving home. That approach also can address other concerns of the young adult; two of these, premarriage and marriage, will be addressed in chapter 4.

Another significant concern is religion, which becomes dominant around the transition age of thirty, when young adulthood is coming to an end. The adult is settling down, and part of settling down is giving attention to the role one will play in the faith drama or story. Concern for one's spiritual roots is present during young adulthood, but the transition age of thirty, generally accompanied by full launching into the world, stimulates the need to give attention to one's spiritual basis.

Pastoral care during this transition age can take on a spiritual orientation. Here the pastor listens to the stories of the adult and helps the person discern God's presence and story working in his or her life. Pastors over age thirty can draw on their own personal experiences of God at that age as a means of facilitating discernment. Stories from others who discerned God's story and presence during the age-thirty transition can also be shared.

## Middle Adulthood as a Life Crisis

Middle adulthood is the period between thirty-five and fifty-five when we begin to decline physically, when we must reorient our dreams in life, and when we must establish a transcendent basis for identity. The major crisis in mid-life is to find one's place in a culture that values youth more than seasoned wisdom. The dominant narrative concern of those in mid-life is the search for a more lasting story and plot that will enable them to transcend a culture that is hostile to aging.

Pastoral care in mid-life is concerned with assisting mid-lifers to discern the appropriate scenario, story, or plot that will form the basis of their character as they face the second half of life. Pastoral care during mid-life helps persons to anchor their lives in a faith story that will enable them to find a lasting basis for self. This narrative basis must be the source of mid-lifers' meaning and purpose. It must give them a sense of making a significant contribution to life, despite unfulfilled dreams, loss of youth, and decreasing significance in the job market.

The needs of a lasting narrative basis in mid-life are

true for both black males and black females. Females, however, may have an advantage over men in resolving the mid-life crisis, since black women, as a whole, have been attending to their need for a religious or spiritual basis for identity throughout adulthood. This gender difference is supported by a culture that expects women to maintain their relatedness with one another and with God. Men, on the other hand, are expected to deny their need for others and for relatedness to God. They are expected to be self-sufficient, to make their way as rugged individualists. As a result, black men lag far behind black women in developing a lasting basis of identity in spiritual sources.

Because black men cannot ignore the need for a spiritual source of identity at mid-life, many do begin to turn toward spiritual things at this stage. They become more concerned about relationships with significant others, about building more lasting relationships with the next generation, about leaving the world a better place for their offspring. Finally, they concern themselves with being better mates to their spouses. In order to accomplish these concerns, they need a transcendent story on which to base their lives.

Black women in mid-life need to shore up the narrative basis of their identity in the faith story. While relatedness is not the major concern, increased concern for making it in the world emerges. This is especially true for those who have given their primary attention to raising children. Once the children are launched, many black women turn their interest toward the work world. But for many black mothers who raise children at the same time they are working outside the home, launching children still presents a real obstacle in mid-life.

Nonmothers and never-married black women also have a need to renew the narrative and spiritual bases of their identities. Like men, their interests may have been predominantly in the work world, but those with no children and those who never married still have a better balance between their work or career identities and their spiritual identities than do black men.

From a narrative perspective, pastoral care to both men and women in mid-life involves helping them return to the stories of childhood, especially the faith stories. The successful outcome of the mid-life crisis comes when mid-lifers rediscover faith stories on which they were raised. Moreover, the care giver will need to help these mid-lifers allow these stories to take initiative in their lives. This means helping them retell the stories of old and to discern how those stories are shaping their lives in the present.

During mid-life, our children are launched, but it is also a time when we must care for the past generation. I am reminded of one middle-aged man who had a successful career and had never paid much attention to his parents, but now he had begun to worry about them. He told me he discovered an increased need to care for his aging parents in a very dramatic way.

He had awakened early one morning with the Scripture Mark 7:7 on his mind. He did not remember ever encountering the verse before, and he ran to his Bible and began to read, beginning with verse 7. He read through to verse 13, and discovered that this verse had to do with honoring mother and father. He did some reading of commentaries at the church library and realized that the meaning of the passage had to do with neglect of one's parents. This helped convince him of his own neglect, made him aware of his deep spiritual roots, and helped him rediscover a neglected part of his spiritual life. He told me that he was committing himself to Bible study and prayer at his church, so that he could further discover a spiritual resource he had encountered when the Scripture passage came to his mind.

Mid-lifers need to talk with someone who understands their needs for a transcendent resource. The care giver's task is to enter peoples' stories and help them see God's story at work in the their lives. If the care givers have been through mid-life, they can share their own stories. If the care givers are younger, telling stories they have encountered about mid-life can be helpful. The basic assumption in the narrative approach to mid-life is that God's story is at work in these peoples' lives, and the care giver's role is to help the mid-lifer become aware of this.

## Older Adulthood as a Life Crisis

The process of developing a long-lasting faith story on which to build one's life is well underway by the time one reaches retirement. For many older adults, this story forms the basis of the identity that will assist them to negotiate the significant losses of growing old: loss of physical and mental capacities, loss of significant others, loss of meaningful work, loss of significance in a child-oriented culture, and loss of income. Yet, with a well-established faith story, elders can find increased possibilities for life fulfillment.

Life review is a natural process used by elders to bring nurture to their lives in the present. Life review is characterized by the elders returning to past events and reliving them in the present through memory. Pastoral care involves assisting this process of life review so that the elder discerns God's story at work in the memory.

I find delight when I talk with our aging church members on my pastoral visits. They often relate significant stories of their lives in the church. I find my own life enriched by their review, and I feel spiritually blessed when I see God's work in their lives. Not only am I blessed as I hear their stories unfold, but they also are blessed, in that their living memories include continued sustenance in God's unfolding story. My role as a pastor is to listen and rejoice.

Older people sometimes bring out pictures as they review their lives, and I encourage them to show the pictures and tell stories related to them. This is a good way to encourage life review; pastoral care through the use of pictures helps aging persons to recover significant memories.

On one occasion I visited an elder who had lost her son about twenty years earlier. The anniversary of his death was near, and she was depressed. I noticed pictures of her son on the mantle, and I asked her to tell me about them. She gently picked up a picture and shed a few tears. Then she began to relate a story about the time the picture was made. The picture reminded her of a time when her son was with her and of the meaningful moments they had together. This recalling of past events enabled her to balance the sad feelings with positive memories. The very act of sharing a story about the picture helped her to come out of her depression.

Sometimes older people have painful memories or concerns about broken relationships with children or significant others. In such instances, stories are not nurturing devices but cause problems to linger. When an elder raises these concerns, pastoral care should involve prayer for hurt memories by asking God, through the power of the Holy Spirit, to make it possible for past relationships to be healed. I often ask God to reveal to an elder how God is working to heal broken relationships. I ask also that the elder be given the wisdom and power to respond to what God is doing to heal past hurts. The goal is to help the elder cooperate with what God is doing to assist in the life-review process. The assumption is that God is at work in the life-review process to bring healing and wholeness.

### The Role of the Pastor as Care Giver in Life Crises

This chapter has explored a narrative approach to selected life crises. The emphasis has been on predictable crises that people encounter throughout life. The role of the pastor has been described as helping those in crises understand what they are experiencing, facilitating the expression of feelings, and helping individuals to mobilize resources for responding to the crisis. Narrative is a helpful resource for both the pastor and lay care giver. As care givers, the pastor and lay person attend to the person's story and find ways to impact the crisis by sharing stories from their own life experiences. Moreover, the care giver functions to help those in crisis discern and attend to the faith story at work in their lives.

#### NOTES

1. Edward P. Wimberly, *A Conceptual Model for Pastoral Care* (Ann Arbor: University [of Michigan] Microfilms, 1976), pp. 69-74.

# CHAPTER IV

# A Narrative Approach to Premarriage, Marriage, and Family Counseling

African American pastors have opportunities to do premarriage, marriage, and family counseling. From a narrative perspective, pastors draw on their own experiences, their experiences of working with others, and the Bible, for stories that can help them facilitate wholeness in marriages and in families. This chapter focuses on premarriage counseling as a predictable life transition, and on marriage and family counseling as crises bring changes within the family that call for new patterns of response.

From a narrative perspective, premarriage counseling is an effort of the engaged couple to fashion a marital narrative out of their own experiences as a couple. "Couple narrative" refers to stories a couple develops, stories that have their roots in the image of the ideal mate which each spouse brings to the marital relationship.[1] During premarriage the couple begins a story history that will be formed through ritualistic rehearsals on a daily basis. "Ritualistic rehearsals" are repetitive activities that form a context for shaping a couple narrative. Taking meals together, attending church, and periodic nights out are examples of ritualistic activities.

Families also have narratives that inform how family members relate. Every family visualizes itself in a particular way. The family has images and themes that influence its behavior. The narrative of the family defines who the family is and how the family behaves.

From a narrative perspective, pastoral care to engaged couples, to married couples, and to families focuses on how pastors and lay people can influence the narrative of couples and families. The emphasis is on care givers who seek to influence the narrative of couples and families by sharing stories from their own lives and experiences.

## Premarriage

Premarriage counseling presents the pastor with an opportunity to explore the personal stories that people bring to marriage. Each person brings images of the ideal mate; each person also brings expectations about parents, in-laws, and siblings. They have expectations regarding adjusting to new friends and relating to old friends. There are also concerns about religious activities and other outside activities. In premarriage counseling from a narrative perspective, the pastor is concerned about the story that each person brings, and in what way the personal stories may impact the couple's relationship.

A major concern of black couples who are considering marriage is that they will leave their families of birth and form a couple narrative. The basic concern is that loyalty will be transferred from one's family-of-origin narrative to a new narrative, a couple narrative. The following approach to premarriage counseling illustrates how one pastor sought to prepare engaged couples for that transition. I am indebted to my own father for this point of view; he often talked about what he did in premarriage counseling.

1. The first question I ask a couple before they get married is, What is the foundation of a happy and enduring home? Of course, some of them come to it almost immediately, and some beat around the bush and never quite answer the question. Some say getting along with each other. Finally, if they do not get it themselves, I tell them.

2. I tell them that the foundation of a happy and enduring marriage is love and loyalty. When things go haywire, then there is something in love and loyalty to fall back on. If they build their marriage on financial considerations alone, for example, there is nothing to support the marriage when the couple suffers hard times.

3. The next question I ask is, Where is your loyalty? In my own pastoral experience, this is where a marriage has its difficulty. Many couples don't know their first loyalty. Some of them say their first loyalty is to their mother. If they are not able to answer the question, I tell them that their first loyalty is to each other, and that they should not let their mothers, fathers, sisters, or brothers come between them as husband and wife. As a couple, they no longer will be two individuals; rather, they will become one. I warn them that their relatives and friends will interfere, and that they must be very sure that their loyalty is to each other.

4. Then I ask them about their finances, to find out the kind of living arrangements they are making, whether they will be living with their parents. I then explain to them the dangers of such an arrangement,

similar to the dangers to young adults from parents and relatives. I tell them it is best to get their own quarters, separate from their parents and relatives, if possible.

5. I try to find out if the couple is aware of the conflicts they will have in marriage. I ask them where they will turn if they have a problem that lasts more than a week, which they cannot solve by sitting down in conversation. Many of them say that they will turn to friends and parents for advice. I warn them that this often causes more harm than good, because parents and relatives take sides. I tell them they need to seek outside help—a pastor who is trained in marriage counseling or a professional counselor. Trained counselors lead you to find your own answers to problems and do not give the wrong (unprofessional) advice.

I have developed this approach to premarriage counseling from my own experience. I have dealt with interference in my own marriage from my relatives, and I have counseled many couples who have had this problem. The biblical reference to couples cleaving to each other and the marriage ritual of my own denomination have been very helpful to me in this area.

## Narrative Reflection

My father once explained to me how he formulated his approach to premarriage counseling. He pointed out the role played by his own experience, as well as his understanding of the Bible and the marriage ritual. His experience and his methods for solving his own difficulties with relatives became the basic sources of his pastoral care, and the Bible and the marriage service gave normative support.

In black pastoral care, it was customary to draw upon personal experience and biblical tradition. That is, my father had no behavioral models to draw upon that were adequate for his needs. His approach is illustrative of inductive guidance in historical pastoral care. "Inductive" pastoral care refers to drawing upon the pastor's and parishioners' own experiences.

My dad was not addressing the narratives of couples directly; rather, he used his own experiences to develop a series of questions to ask engaged couples. These questions, however, served to reveal the nature of the personal narrative that each person brought to the marriage. I have often heard my dad say that many soon-to-be-married couples brought to marriage a story that had as its foundation primary loyalty to one's family of birth. He indicated he knew that this would lead to marital conflict, so he sought to address primary loyalties right away. Not only would he use his own struggles in early marriage as an example, but he would bring into the counseling biblical references to leaving mother and father and cleaving only to one's own mate. In this way he was seeking to lay the groundwork for the man and woman to fashion a new couple narrative.

## Marriage

Pastoral care to couples during crisis relates to the way the couple narrative sustains and nurtures the couple in times of difficulty. When a couple faces obstacles that cannot be resolved through the customary resources, the pastor's role is to help them bring their couple narrative to bear on the crisis. Sometimes the narrative is adequate, and sometimes it is not, so the role of the pastor is to assess the narrative and its potential use in crisis. If the couple narrative is adequate and capable of sustaining the couple, the pastor facilitates its use; if it is inadequate, the pastor must help the couple to edit it.

As previously indicated, a couple narrative is a story that a married couple fashion together, a story rooted in the image of the ideal spouse which each spouse brings to the marriage. A healthy couple narrative is one that the couple has revised, so that each spouse's ideal-spouse image is based upon a realistic image of the actual spouse. This more realistic narrative recognizes the strengths and weaknesses of each spouse, so that each acts with the other in realistic ways. The unhealthy couple narrative is one in which either one or both spouses maintain the ideal-spouse image, in spite of the realistic nature of the spouses; this narrative supports unrealistic behavior toward one or both spouses that is frustrating and destructive.

One of the primary couple narratives relates to the way a couple handles differentness. Differentness is rooted in the fact that each person in a marital relationship is different and unique. A healthy couple narrative is rooted in the realization that the spouses are different, and the narrative supports each spouse's differentness. An unhealthy narrative ignores that differentness and seeks to force each spouse into the other's ideal-spouse image, without regard for the uniqueness or differentness of the actual spouse. The role of the care giver is to help the couple with a healthy narrative to bring it to bear on a crisis. When the couple has an unhealthy narrative, the goal of the care givers is to help them edit this narrative by enabling each spouse to accept the differentness of the other.

The following example of a healthy couple narrative

is based on the realization that two people do not need to be in agreement to have a good marital relationship. This couple's ability to resolve crises within their relationship was rooted in their view of themselves as a couple and in the way they were able to accept their personal differences. Their need was to realize that each spouse had a different religious disposition. Each was raised in a different denomination and had different levels of comfort in terms of worship preference. One spouse was Baptist and preferred informal and spontaneous worship with emotional expressiveness. The other spouse was raised in an Episcopal tradition and preferred more form with less spontaneity. They had experimented for a long time and found that they could not find a happy medium. A crisis developed when the couple realized that they could not comfortably modify their personal orientations. They felt that this differentness would lead to a marital split, since both had believed "a family that worships together, stays together."

The pastor who intervened discovered that they had developed a couple-worship style of prayer, song, and Bible reading. They did this daily and found it very satisfying. The pastor supported their private family worship as appropriate and told them that this qualified as the kind of worship that met their beliefs. The pastor also indicated that the storied life they would develop in private couple worship could sustain them, despite their preference for different types of public worship. The pastor also shared several stories of successful couples who attended different churches throughout their married life because of personal preferences. The pastor emphasized, however, that couple private worship rituals were important to foster because of their apparent differentness and preference.

The pastor was able to use a constructive couple narrative history of worship, as well as several stories from his own experience, to help the couple resolve their difficulty. However, not every couple in crisis has a storied history of supporting spousal differentness. In fact, some couples cannot resolve a crisis because of the inability to accept individual differences.

I am reminded of a couple in which the husband had a particular preference in terms of homemaking. During courtship, his wife-to-be raised no real opposition to his expectations. Both were college graduates, but the husband expected his wife to suppress her career and professional goals. After a year of marriage, the wife's career goals surfaced. At first the husband ignored them, and when his wife quietly persisted, a crisis developed. The husband's ideal image of a wife was challenged. He made several unsuccessful efforts to force his wife to conform to his expected ideal image. He would not support her career goals and would reinforce only behavior that related to the traditional role of the housewife. When this lack of support became unbearable, the couple went to the pastor. The husband expected the pastor to reinforce a particular biblical view of the husband as the head of the household and the wife as helpmate; the wife hoped the pastor would remain more open and help them work through the crisis.

The pastor realized the crisis was one of differentness. Apparently both had an implied or implicit agreement about marital roles, but after marriage the wife no longer was happy with the contract. She felt the contract was detrimental, and she wanted to renegotiate. Because the pastor recognized the need to

respect the wife's emerging professional career identity and the husband's need to accept his wife's
emerging sense of self, he began to explore a biblical
image of mutuality because of the couple's rootedness
in a biblical understanding of marriage.

Using Ephesians 5:21-33, the pastor emphasized
verses 21, 25, and 28, indicating that this was a
passage of mutuality, where the true head of the house
was one who created an environment where all family
members could grow. The husband found the passage
interesting, but he was reluctant to buy into the
pastor's interpretation.

The pastor realized that the crisis would not be
resolved immediately and began to lay the foundation
for helping the couple move toward a narrative history
which included acceptance of differences. He told a
story about a husband and wife who accepted a
biblical interpretation of nonmutual family headship,
pointing out that this interpretation remained dominant for years, until one day the couple discovered that
they had grown into mutuality. After telling this story,
the pastor asked the couple to reflect on it while they
set aside several sessions to discuss the marital crisis.

By using a Bible passage as well as a story from his
own experience, the pastor helped the couple begin to
edit their own narrative. The pastor understood the
psychological principle of differentness, as well as the
theological principle of mutuality in marital relationships, and he used these principles in a narrative
model to help the couple in their crisis.

## Family

Crisis in family life occurs when the family as a
whole faces obstacles that cannot be resolved with its
ordinary methods of problem solving. Normally,

families have patterns that help the members to function. Husbands and wives find ways to respond to each other; parents find ways to raise children; and children find ways to relate to their parents and to one another. Whether these ways of relating are healthy or unhealthy, the family rarely questions these patterns until a crisis develops. Then the customary patterns are challenged, and the family seeks to recover these patterns as much as possible.

Often a family turns to its pastor when there is a crisis, needing help to restore the family to its former customary functioning. Then the pastor must assess whether the family is living a healthy story and determine how to use the family story, if it is healthy, as a resource in resolving the crisis; or the pastor must help the family to edit its unhealthy story.

A healthy family has a realistic story that will help it respond to a crisis. An unhealthy family has a story that designates someone within the family to blame for the crisis, which results in a faulty crisis resolution. In other words, a healthy family story enables the family to face the problem head on and support each family member emotionally during the crisis, but an unhealthy family story designates one family member as the cause of the problem. The end result is that the rest of the family lives at the expense of another family member.

The role of the care giver in counseling a family with a healthy story is to enable that story to sustain the family until the crisis is resolved. An example of such a family story is one in which the members genuinely care for one another and reinforce their emotional ties when facing obstacles. The role of the pastor is to help family members care for one another as they face the crisis.

A healthy family scenario is one that says, "We can handle anything as long as we stick together and continue to care for one another." I heard of one such family, in which the father was laid off because of cutbacks at the factory. Fortunately, he received some severance and vacation pay and also was eligible for unemployment compensation. All the family members sat down and looked at the family financial needs and discovered they could make it for about three months before they felt a real financial crunch.

The pastor visited the family to see if they needed help. The whole family, including two children and the husband's mother, welcomed the pastor. When the pastor indicated that he was especially concerned about the family's financial and emotional strength, he discovered they had already made survival plans that included a slight modification in spending and the postponement of purchases until they were financially able. The children knew that things would be hard, that they would not have money for things that were not essential. The husband admitted that at first he had been really worried, but when he had faced the family with the reality, the members had responded that they had weathered worse storms in the past, and they felt they had the resources to handle this crisis.

After listening to their story and how they had marshaled their resources as a family, the pastor affirmed the positive family story and told them about how the early church had surrounded Peter with prayer when he was arrested. He indicated that the entire church would be praying for the family, just as it had prayed for Peter. When the pastor left, he knew this family was facing its crisis with a positive story; they had the necessary resources to face the problem and resolve it. His role was to reinforce the existing resources and to use the faith story to reinforce the positive family resources. He wanted to communicate to the family that God's story also was sustaining them and that they had support from a caring congregation.

Sometimes families with negative stories will label one family member as the cause of a family problem. The role of the pastor in such a situation is to help the family modify its negative story so that it can better resolve the crisis. The pastor can tell stories that help the family face the problems head on, rather than designate one member as the cause. The following example illustrates this well.

The family (which we will call the Jones family, consisting of Esther, age 30; George, 34; and four children: two boys, ages 6 and 8; two girls, ages 9 and 11) still lived in a small apartment in the home of George's mother at the time of the intervention. Esther and George had been married eleven years. Esther was a housewife, and George worked for the city and also was in partnership with several friends in a clothing store. His pay was barely enough to make ends meet.

George was extremely close to his mother and was inclined to accept her advice, rather than his wife's, concerning the needs of the children. Being the landlady, George's mother felt that she had the right to enter the Jones' home whenever she deemed it necessary, and her intrusions formed the basis for constantly recurring fights between George and Esther. The involvement of Esther's family was evidenced by the fact that her four brothers and sisters often cared for the children when Esther needed to rest.

Violent arguments erupted among all family members. On the one hand, Esther and George engaged in arguments that eventuated in threats and counter-threats concerning divorce, money, and the children. Such disputes were never resolved, thus their problems seemed to worsen rather than become better. On the other hand, the children also engaged in arguments that evolved into pushing and shoving, resulting in a high noise level which caused Esther to shout at them. Moreover, the children often became involved in parental disagreements, particularly those that centered around them. In these instances, the children often became pawns whom Esther and George used against each other.

Outside the home, the boys were discipline problems, although the girls appeared to be model children. The acting-out behavior of the boys caused difficulty in school, and both parents consequently made frequent visits there. Though the girls did not exhibit the same problematic behavior, they nonetheless lacked initiative and constantly depended upon others for guidance.

Esther went to the pastor, complaining that she feared George had become involved with another woman. The pastor had observed the great deal of tension that existed in the family and was glad Esther was seeking aid. After he listened to Esther's story, he decided he needed to talk to the husband before trying to determine the cause of the problem. When he visited the home and talked to the husband, to each child, and to the mother-in-law, the pastor discovered that the children became involved in the marital arguments. Their story was that they were concerned that their father might become violent with their mother, although they felt that their mother was too nagging and should back off. They also told him that they would intervene to try to lessen the loud shouting and bring some degree of reason to the situation.

When the pastor realized that this was a true family crisis that would require long-term counseling and that he did not have the time or the skill to take on the problem, he approached the family about referring them to a family counselor. There was a great deal of resistance from both George and Esther. George believed the problem was Esther's fault; he felt she didn't know how to raise children or make a home inviting for a man. Esther believed the problem was George's fault; she felt he was a mamma's boy who let his mother make all the decisions. Each felt that family counseling would be of no value because the problem was the other spouse's problem.

The pastor's goal became one of preparing the couple for referral to family counseling. The pastor felt that several sessions were necessary for the family to realize that there were serious problems within the family that could not be blamed on any one individual. The pastor decided that both George and Esther must get beyond blaming the other if they were to focus on the real problem, which was that they had not developed their own relationship as husband and wife. Rather, they had allowed unnecessary intrusions from their children and from George's mother to affect their relationship and the raising of their children.

The pastor sought to lay the groundwork by telling a story from his own life. He told the couple about a problem his daughter once had in school. He said that he and his wife had blamed each other for the problem, with charges and countercharges. Then one day, the daughter had shouted that both of them were the problem, because they never could come to any common understanding about anything. The pastor indicated that that was the first time he and his wife had realized that the problem was in their relationship and that blaming each other was not solving anything.

Of course, Esther and George did not fully understand this story, but the foundation for an effective referral had been laid. Scapegoating, or each spouse blaming the other for their relational problem, was identified by the pastor as the major obstacle in the development of an effective family environment. The pastor sought the use of narrative to address the need of the family for family counseling.

## Role of the Pastor in Counseling Couples and Families

The pastor uses narrative pastoral care in premarriage, marriage, and family counseling with African American people, to support the positive use of narrative stories in the handling of life crises. Moreover, by telling stories from their own experiences, as well as stories from the experiences of others, care givers can help couples and families with negative narratives to edit and revise their narratives. The goal of such storytelling is to enable the couple or family to face the crisis and resolve it.

### NOTES

1. See Dennis A. Bagarozzi and Stephen A. Andersen, *Personal, Marital, and Family Myths* (New York: W. W. Norton, 1989).

# CHAPTER V

# Personal Resources for Developing a Narrative Approach

The narrative approach to pastoral care in the black church has been defined as drawing upon personal experience and the Bible for stories that might facilitate caring for those in need. Critically important to this process are several important skills. A major skill is the pastor's ability to have an "approachable," or perhaps "integrating," and conflict-free source for storytelling. This chapter explores the personal resources in a pastor's life that can offer a conflict- and anxiety-free source of narrative.

## Conflict-free Storytelling

Conflict-free storytelling refers to stories from the pastor's life and experience which have been so sufficiently worked through emotionally that the pastor can tell them without fear. In other words, the pastor can tell them without stirring up unresolved problems in his or her life that still need therapeutic attention. The anxiety-free storyteller is often a wounded healer whose own wounds have been sufficiently addressed, so that the stories emerging from the healing of personal wounds can be used as narrative. The storyteller should be one whose wounds have been healed to the extent that his or her story can be a source of another's healing.

A conflict-free storyteller also is aware of the major areas of ongoing personal conflict. There are areas in a pastor's close relationships and interactions with people that can continue to present problems. The pastor not only must be aware of these areas, but also must be able to keep these ongoing problems from interfering with the facilitative ways he or she relates to the needs of others. A conflict-free storyteller is aware of ongoing problems in life and has found ways to prevent them from intruding into caring for others.

The major question is whether there are indigenous patterns within the black church where pastors can work together naturally to develop their abilities so as to be at ease with themselves as storytellers. There are natural settings where ministers gather to tell stories. The major concern in developing anxiety-free and conflict-free stories is finding a place where the pastor can tell *personal* stories. Following are examples of some ways pastors can involve themselves in telling personal stories, in order to become conflict-free storytellers.

Since we assume that storytelling is the basic method of learning within the black culture, the implication is that black pastors must be able to share and reflect on the stories they tell, for the purpose of visualizing their healing value for themselves and others. They must have a setting in which they can tell stories to one another and, through this sharing, resolve personal anxiety as well as become conflict-free in their own minds. Such a setting needs to involve a trained specialist whom the pastors can draw on as a resource for personal healing as well as for counseling skills.

## Birth Mythology

One potential area of anxiety and conflict for pastors may be in the area of birth mythology. "Birth mythology" refers to the stories pastors hear about their own birth. Sometimes these stories are an important source of nurture and growth; for other pastors, they are a present source of anxiety. But whether they are positive sources of identity and nurture or sources of anxiety, there needs to be a setting where these stories can be retold so that they no longer are threatening.

A brief review of the nature of birth mythology is helpful in explaining how these stories can be nurturing or threatening. Birth mythology is composed of the stories one hears from parents and relatives concerning the circumstances surrounding one's birth. These circumstances include specific periods in the birth process, such as conception, time in the womb, the actual birth, the first months of life, and the religious dedication or infant baptism. Critical questions can help trigger the remembrance of the birth mythology in an adult: (1) What were the circumstances surrounding your conception? (2) Were you planned or unplanned? (3) What dreams and expectations did your parents have for you before you were born? (4) What was the first thing your mother said when she first saw you? (5) What did your father say when he first saw you? (6) What was life like the first year you were born? (7) When, where, and why were you dedicated or baptized as an infant?

Of course, these questions can be answered only by parents, and what they say forms the basis of the birth mythology. That is to say, what we hear about our birth and the circumstances surrounding it are the foundation from which birth mythology springs. These stories are the roots of personal identity, as well as the primary sources of a child's God image.[1]

One illustration of a birth-mythology narrative is this story, told by one pastor to another:

> One of the earliest stories told about my life as a baby concerns how God used my mother and heard the prayers of the righteous to save me from a life-threatening condition.
>
> My mother became concerned about my "turning blue" and cries of pain when I was placed on my back. She also observed a growth on my head. Upon examining me, the doctor dismissed her concerns, saying she probably had dropped me on my head and that I really wasn't blue. I was pronounced normal and sent home.
>
> Mom persisted and brought me back repeatedly, traveling with her new son (her third child) on the bus in the cold Chicago winter, while her grandmother took care of my older sister and brother. On one such occasion, after one doctor, an intern, had told her that she had nothing to worry about, an experienced nurse stood behind the doctor and listened to his erroneous diagnosis.
>
> She said, "Lady, I'm not supposed to contradict the doctor, but he's just an intern and doesn't know what he is talking about. If you will bring your son back here tomorrow morning, I will make sure that he sees a specialist." The next morning, that specialist determined that there was a growth, and it was a sign of a dangerous blood clot that was moving toward my brain. When I was put on my back, more blood flowed to my head and caused me severe pain. My "turning blue" was a result of this condition. I'm told

that he gave me shots that very day to attempt to calcify the clot. The saints prayed that I would be healed and that I would not suffer brain damage. I look back on this story of my healing and on other occasions in which I could have lost my life, and I believe that God has given me the gift of life for a special purpose.

This pastor visualized from the stories told him that he was created for some special purpose. Through these stories, he was able to sense that he was a child of destiny and that his destiny was tied to God in some way. This gave him a sense of "somebodiness" as well as laying the foundation for his acceptance of a call to ministry. Moreover, he learned very early that there was a God who responded to people's prayers.

This pastor also envisaged a connection between the early stories he heard from his mother and the way they influenced his general outlook on life and his ministry. He saw suffering as part of life, but he sensed God's presence in the midst of life's difficulties.

He said, "By and large, people are still subject to problems of human existence. God is behind the dynamic force which both sustains and liberates people in the midst of suffering. Though healing and wholeness are possible with God, ultimate healing by God is found beyond time."

This birth mythology was a conflict-free and anxiety-free story which affected the pastor's outlook on life. It influenced everything he did from birth to the present. He saw it as a positive influence and as a positive source for his ministry, and because it was conflict- and anxiety-free, he was able to draw on it when necessary in caring for others.

Birth mythology is not always positive, however.

There are situations when birth mythology is negative, and this negativity has a pejorative influence on the person's outlook on life. For example, one woman had a call to ministry, but because of the circumstances surrounding her birth, she had difficulty seeing herself as a minister. She had a feeling very early in her life that she was not a wanted child. When she began to wonder about the circumstances that surrounded her life, she found that her parents were in the midst of some serious marital problems when she was conceived. She felt that this had a deleterious impact on her existence, and she saw life through pessimistic lenses, feeling worthless. She managed to get herself into awkward situations where people would take advantage of her kindness, and consequently, she felt inadequate and hesitated to give a full commitment to ministry.

Fortunately, she told this story in a supportive group of pastors, who responded with concern and support. The sharing situation gave the pastors a chance to affirm her gifts and to support her—to attend her birth mythology. So that her birth mythology could become an anxiety- and conflict-free source of storytelling, they encouraged her to use the group, as well as other supportive caring and counseling resources, to help her become a wounded healer.

All pastors are wounded healers. Some have conflict- and anxiety-free birth mythologies; many do not. Yet sharing birth mythologies in supportive environments can provide a first step in becoming a wounded healer, with a conflict- and anxiety-free mind. Having integrated one's own personal birth mythology into one's life, whether good or bad, one can then share that story with those in need.

## Childhood Stories, Roles, and Relationships

Another source of stories are those with which pastors identified as children. In these stories one can find sources for resolving conflict- and anxiety-laden problems that a child faces. Returning to these stories can be an excellent source of conflict-free narratives.

One pastor, as a child, identified with Moses in the Exodus story, and this story provided an early vision of what life should be like for African American people. He said, "Moses was a favorite because I learned to identify my own fight for justice through the Exodus story, and I was taught not to accept injustice. I saw very early the plight of black people through the eyes of the story of Moses and God's people."

Another pastor identified with other characters of the Bible who helped him gain important perspectives for developing a purpose in life:

> I also liked David, because of the way he grew from being a little shepherd boy in the fields to prominence. As a young boy, I always found the whole story of David very fascinating. I learned that God could use very young people for God's purposes. I looked forward to the day when I could know what God wanted me to do with my life, because of what I saw God doing through David.

This same pastor also said that he liked the stories of Paul:

> Paul's conversation showed me that God would nurture and care for you as you moved into being a Christian. It showed that becoming a Christian was a growth process. I always had a sense of hope because of Paul. Through him, I knew I

*87*

could continue to grow and be Christian, even
though it seemed all those around me felt that
becoming Christian happened all at once. Paul
did have a sudden conversion, but he also lived
his life in such a way that you could see how he
also grew after the conversion.

Other pastors have identified with stories that
helped them grow as children and youths, in spite of
the obstacles. One pastor pointed out the importance
of the three Hebrew boys in his growth process:

When I was very young, I liked stories that were a
challenge to me. I liked Shadrach, Meshach, and
Abednego. I also liked to hear about Jesus
teaching in the temple when he was only twelve
years old. Shadrach and his friends, as youths,
risked death for what they believed. And Jesus at
the temple showed that at a young age, individuals could do some awesome stuff.

As a child, I too was inspired by Bible stories, and
by stories of my father's days at Bethune-Cookman
college—when it was a two-year college and Bethune
had just merged with Cookman. My father often
mentioned the faith of Mary McLeod Bethune. He
proudly told how she built a black college on faith in
God and how she knew that God would come through
when money and resources for the institution were
scarce. He also talked about her favorite story in the
Bible—Esther—and how she saw herself and her
mission through the story of Esther. From the stories
my father told of Mary McLeod Bethune, I learned the
importance of faith in life, particularly when working
for God on behalf of your race.

African American women pastors also have found
Bible stories important in shaping their identities.

One female pastor in a pentecostal denomination could not recall one favorite Bible story, but she indicated that thinking of herself as a person in ministry began when she encountered God in a vision early in her life. After feeling God's spirit move in her, she said that Esther became very important to her. Her orientation was toward God's movement in her life, and she sought to understand and interpret God's movement and presence through the use of Bible stories.

Another ordained pastor identified with the message of particular books of the Bible, rather than with particular characters. This pastor liked Exodus very early in her life, because of its liberation themes. She saw God as the major actor in Exodus, leading God's people to freedom. She also liked the Gospel of Luke and the letter to the Galatians. In Luke, she saw God respecting every person, whether male or female, slave or free. God and Jesus Christ were concerned with the least of those in society.

Many pastors I have interviewed identified, in their childhood, with stories and characters who helped them envision possibilities for their growth and development as persons. Some found that the perspective of the early stories carried them through their ministries. Those early stories became part of their lives and a ready resource for stories that were anxiety- and conflict-free. They had positive plots, meaning that they had a positive direction, which facilitated personal growth. And because those plots led the pastors toward even further growth and development, they were also sources of anxiety- and conflict-free narratives.

At times, stories that pastors identify with are not helpful. I think of one pastor who identified with the

Greek mythological character Sisyphus.[2] In Hades, Sisyphus was sentenced forever to roll a stone up a hill. Each time the stone almost reached the top of the hill, it became too heavy and rolled back down, and Sisyphus would have to begin all over again.

For the pastor who identified with the tragic figure of Sisyphus to become a wounded healer, he would need to find the kind of experiences that would help him edit this story which was shaping his life, a story which was not anxiety- or conflict-free. Some experiences had contributed to this view of life as a series of tragic, repeated endings and painful restarts, and this tragic scenario needed to be told in a caring storytelling environment, where it could be edited by feedback from supportive others. In its Greek mythological form, the story was inadequate for use in ministry; in order to use it as a positive resource in its edited form, the pastor would need to undergo some caring intervention.

Early role playing, when a child takes on certain roles and functions within the home, can become a rich resource for anxiety- and conflict-free stories. One example is a woman who was an active participant in the life of her father's church. She had a speaking engagement in this church even as a little girl; as a preteen she often gave a speech or read a poem, and members of the congregation would respond with such comments as, "You really preached today!" This pastor had long talks with her father about the reaction of the congregation, and he was very supportive of her role in the life of the church. As a result of the support she received, she indicated that at an early age, she knew that her life was not her own, but that it belonged to God: "I can't remember not knowing God. But during my teenage years I started wrestling with the thought of what I would do with my life, about what God wanted me to do. All through college I wrestled with the idea of ministry. Consciously, I was not ready, but subconsciously, I was preparing for it."

This woman played significant roles within the life of the church. The support of others, and especially that of her father, contributed to building a faith structure which later matured when she decided to go into ministry.

Sometimes the roles played in childhood are not as positive as the one just cited. Negative roles, particularly those in which a child must assume adult responsibility prematurely, can become sources of anxiety and conflict. In such cases, it is the task of the wounded healers to gain sufficient separation from the negative roles so that they can freely choose an action response different from the negative role. And a caring and loving environment of support is required in order to gain the ability to choose. When persons find themselves free from the negative roles, then as wounded healers, they can draw on those personal stories when caring for others.

Other significant sources of anxiety- and conflict-free stories are the relationships pastors had with those who were close to them early in their lives. An anxiety- and conflict-free relationship is one in which genuine care is offered by those concerned. One example is a female pastor who admired her minister father, not only because he supported her in her desire to be a minister, but because he was a model father who built a positive relationship with her. He made himself available and was there when she needed him.

Positive relationships with mentors led some pastors to identify with the lives of their mentors and the stories they lived and told. Many pastors found a sense of self-esteem and worth in such relationships. This exchange and sharing of stories became a conflict-free reservoir for them. Not only did some pastors form positive relationships with their mentors, but many learned to tell stories with which their mentors identified. This meant that the pastors told stories they learned from their mentors, which ultimately helped them to learn the narrative approach to life and ministry. But even when relationships with significant others were not good, many pastors found positive relationships with others within the church which more than made up for the tension that existed with some. Pastors have listed Christian teachers, coaches, and lay people as persons who had positive influences on them.

## The Pastor's Resources

The narrative context of the pastor's formative years, the birth mythology that surrounds the pastor's birth, the stories with which the pastor identifies early in life, the roles the pastor plays in life, and the quality of relationships with significant others—all contribute to the development of a reservoir of healing, facilitative, conflict- and anxiety-free stories. But even when these areas are not conflict-free, they can be changed as the result of care and support from significant others, and such support enables the pastor to transform these areas into a reservoir for healing and caring. Through the transformation of the pastor's life, roles, stories, and relationships, he or she becomes a wounded healer with a reservoir of important stories.

Just as doctors should first "heal themselves," so pastors must support and help one another in a healing process, creating personal narratives that can be used to enlighten other narratives, told by someone in need. The role of professional specialists and trainers in pastoral care and counseling is a must in helping the lives of pastors become conflict- and anxiety-free sources of stories.

### NOTES

1. Dennis A. Bagarozzi and Stephen A. Anderson, *Personal, Marital, and Family Myths* (New York: W. W. Norton, 1989), pp. 22-41.

2. For the details of the case, see Edward P. Wimberly, "Spiritual Formation in Theological Education and Psychological Assessment," *Clergy Assessment and Career Development*, ed. Richard A. Hung, John E. Hinkle, and H. Newton Malony (Nashville: Abingdon Press, 1990), pp. 30-31.

# CHAPTER VI

# Indigenous Pastoral Care

## Facing the Twenty-first Century

Because African American oral culture has always used sharing stories in caring situations, this will remain a dominant approach in the African American church. However, the storytelling approaches that are emerging in counseling psychology might prove helpful to this indigenous approach in the future.

The spontaneous use of stories triggered in counseling relies on the right-brain processes of the care giver's thinking. That is to say, the storytelling approach presented in this book relies heavily on the intuitive and imaginative capacities of the pastor or lay person, which are cultivated in oral cultures. Oral cultures emphasize emotion, celebration, poetic expression, relationships, storytelling, and story listening.[1]

The focus of the model presented here is on stories that come spontaneously to the mind of the pastor or lay person, at the actual point of encounter with people or parishioners in need. The emphasis has been on telling stories that emerge as a result of what people are saying. That is, the pastors or lay people tell stories—from their own lives, from their ministries, and from the Bible—that emerge because of something being experienced by those in need. The stories being told, therefore, are spontaneous events that emerge out of a reservoir of stories that are triggered in the encounter with the person in need. This triggering is an unconscious process, in which the person in need has an impact upon the care giver, and the stories that emerge from the care giver are shared with the person in need, in facilitative ways that enable the person to grow.

An indigenous storytelling approach to pastoral care is learned by participating and living in an oral community, where hearing and speaking are very central. However, it cannot be taken for granted that this approach will remain viable and alive without some intentional effort. The more the dominant culture becomes visual, a seeing, reading, and writing culture, the greater the likelihood that oral indigenous approaches will lose some of their influence. This chapter is an attempt to review some of the present literature on storytelling in counseling, and its implication for an indigenous approach to pastoral care in the black church in the twenty-first century.

## Other Related Models

The new therapeutic approaches to storytelling rely on assessment of the caring needs of persons from the perspectives of developmental psychology and personality theory. These approaches use psychological theories of counseling, in conjunction with theories of human growth, to suggest how to use storytelling. In addition, some storytelling theories outline complex structures which match the story to the phase of counseling and the need of the person.

One model focuses on sharing stories at particular

points in the counseling process.[2] These specific points include the goal-setting stage, the stage of focusing on specific developmental problems and behavioral problems, and the stage of family problems. The goal of the use of stories in this model is to evoke ideas, feelings, attitudes, and attention to relationships that might facilitate the counseling. This approach also outlines specific steps in story creation that reflect the specific problem being addressed.

Another approach assumes that people rework unresolved conflict by acting out specific themes in stories.[3] The goal in this approach is to affect the themes that people are acting out in resolving problems by helping the counselees identify the actual story themes that are related to conflict. Once these themes are identified, counselors design strategies for influencing the stories that have given rise to the conflicts. The goal of influencing these stories is to help the counselees develop more growth-facilitative themes, myths, and self-definitions. Storytelling is a major means of influencing the existing stories and themes in the counselee's life.

Still another storytelling model designs stories based on treatment goals.[4] In this goal-oriented approach, once the goals for counseling are set, counselors explore their experience for stories similar to those of the counselees. When these are identified in the counselor's life, stories are constructed to help achieve the goals that have been set. This approach relies on protocols, or carefully structured stories to meet the goals of the counseling. These protocols focus on the development of stories around characters, relationships, movements, feelings, or behaviors.

In addition to these varied approaches in therapy, there are also various approaches to Bible storytelling.

One such approach focuses on structuring stories based on the natural rhythm of the story.[5] This helps the pastor and lay person construct biblical stories based on the internal structure of the story itself.

## A Goal-oriented Model

All these approaches have implications for an indigenous storytelling approach to pastoral care as we face the twenty-first century. They suggest that one specific direction lies in preplanning stories, and they offer specifics for ways this can be done. There is some value to preplanning stories, even if one does not have an opportunity to use them, since one can build one's repertoire of stories, to be drawn on when needed. Second, preplanning can increase the storytelling facility of the care giver, so that when stories are told, they can be more useful to those in need of care.

The approach I want to emphasize is the goal-oriented approach—addressing a particular counseling goal through the use of story. In this approach, counselors first identify the goal and then begin to explore their own experience to discover a story similar to that of the counselee. When such a story is identified, the process of building a story for counseling begins.

Although the goal-oriented model is a preplanning model, it focuses on the personal experiences and life of the counselor, so this approach actually is similar to the indigenous approach to storytelling described in this book. The goal-oriented model can serve as a method for constructing stories that can be used in counseling as well as in other settings. While the indigenous storytelling approach grows naturally out of an oral culture, one can rehearse and build stories in many settings within an oral culture, and the goal-oriented model lends itself to those natural occasions.

The central building block for the goal-oriented model is the protocol—a standard procedure, a map, a set of guidelines—which can be followed in building a story to facilitate the accomplishment of a particular goal. When building a story with the protocol method, the counselor must have in mind the goal that the story needs to address. The goal could involve attitudes that need challenging, feelings that need to be expressed, some behavior that needs to be enhanced or modified, a perspective that needs to be impacted, or some decision that needs to be made.[6] Once the goal has been identified, the counselors can plumb their own experiences for stories that are possibilities for story building to meet the goal.

The protocol for building stories usually has several steps. The first phase is the exploration of the presenting problem, the initial concern that has led the person to counseling at this particular time.

Once the problem is presented within its social and interpersonal context, general information is gathered. This second phase includes helping the counselee gain a larger perspective of the presenting problem by exploring it from various psychological assessment models. This phase usually ends when counseling goals are established, based on assessment of the needs of the counselee. These goals, agreed upon between the counselor and the counselee, include the problem the counselee desires to address in the counseling—the desired changes in feelings, attitude, perspective, behavior, and identity that the person wants to accomplish.

The third phase begins when the goals are set and the counseling process moves toward accomplishing the established goals.[7] In this phase, pastoral counselors turn their attention to the unfolding story of the counselee. If the need for storytelling arises, counselors need to have in mind the steps for building a story based on the protocol:

Step 1: Explore their own lives and situations for stories that might be similar to the desired goals that have been established.

Step 2: Choose a main character, or several main characters, who have problems and goals similar to those of the counselee.

Step 3: Choose a character or situation and build a story, developing in detail the character and/or situation that introduces the desired changes required by the counseling goal. The key is to stimulate the imagination of the listener.

Step 4: Explore in detail the consequences for the main characters in achieving or not achieving the desired goals. This step must show that there are consequences in accomplishing or not accomplishing the desired goals.

The protocol helps pastoral counselors develop stories based on the established counseling goals. It also helps the storyteller develop specific characters, contexts, and plots that can trigger the imagination of the counselee. It must be emphasized that learning to tell stories in this way requires training and supervision in basic counseling skills, including building rapport, empathy, assessment of psychological and interpersonal dynamics, and the phases of counseling. Such training should be in the form of courses, as well as in actual practice and in reflection on that practice with experienced trainers. Training will enhance pastors' ability to deliver quality care to parishioners, as well as strengthen the pastors' own personal and emotional growth.

Following is one example of the use of a protocol to develop a story to achieve a certain counseling goal. This example contains the three protocol steps: (1) It addresses a perspective that must be changed, challenged, or explored in the main character's life; (2) It introduces an opposite perspective through a different character; (3) It relates the consequences of each character's perspectives.[8]

I once counseled a man who had a very negative outlook on life. He felt his life was doomed, that there was no hope for him. Laboring under the weight of difficult memories, he saw very little chance to undo their impact. As he talked, the Bible story of Joseph's betrayal by his brothers came to me. I decided to take some time to read that story again and plan a protocol for telling the story to the counselee at a later date, with his need in mind. The goal was to address his gloom-and-doom perspective and help him envision possibilities in the midst of difficulty. When we met for our next appointment, I related this story:

> Two people were reading the story of Joseph in the book of Genesis. The first person read that Joseph was his father's favorite son, and the father loved him so much that he made him a special coat. Joseph's brothers saw how their father treated him and were very jealous. They decided that all their lives would be different if Joseph were not around, so they seized an opportunity and put him into a deep well where he would never be found.
>
> However, when some slave traders came by, the brothers decided to rescue him from the well and sell him into slavery. They took Joseph's coat

and dipped it in the blood of an animal they had killed. Then they took the bloodied coat to their father and told him that Joseph had been torn apart by an animal. The father was grief stricken, but Joseph was no longer around to anger his brothers by receiving their father's favored treatment.

The first person who read this account became depressed and put the book down. He refused to read any further, pointing out that life was nothing but a bunch of disappointments and that people, particularly family members, will betray you and keep on abusing you. He stopped reading, feeling that the plot had ended and Joseph was doomed to an endless life of slavery.

The second reader did not stop reading when Joseph was sold into slavery. She had a feeling that the story was unfolding chapter by chapter, and it would be too bad to stop reading before the entire story was finished. She made up her mind to follow the story episode by episode, until she came to the dramatic end.

The next episode picked up after Joseph had been in slavery for some time. He was found to be a good and faithful manager. He came to the attention of the ruler, who put Joseph in charge of all his household and domestic affairs.

The second reader noticed that Joseph had made the best of an unfortunate situation. Although he had been abused by his brothers and treated inhumanly, he was able to become indispensable to the new ruler.

The story continued with the introduction of the ruler's wife, who had noticed that Joseph was handsome and very strong. She had a romantic interest in him and made several unsuccessful attempts to get him to go to bed with her. Joseph was a very responsible person who had been entrusted with the entire household. He refused her advances, telling her that such action would undermine the trust which her husband had placed in him. But she would not take no for an answer. She clutched at him. With a quick maneuver he was free from her grasp, but she had grabbed his coat. Then, with coat in hand, she called her attendants and reported that Joseph had attacked her.

The second reader was very disappointed with the way this episode had turned out. An unfortunate event had caused the story to take a different turn. The plot thickened, and the positive became negative. The second reader wanted to stop reading. She had become discouraged, but she decided to read on, realizing that the story was not quite over.

In the next episode, the ruler cast Joseph into prison. Part of the difficulty between Joseph and his brothers in the beginning was caused by a dream he had interpreted to his brothers. In the dream, he was ruling over his brothers. Of course, his brothers resented this, and one consequence of his arrogance was that he was sold into slavery. The point of this brief interpretative interlude is that Joseph was a dreamer and an interpreter of dreams. And eventually, it was this God-given talent that became the central element in Joseph's prison life.

Confined with Joseph while he was in prison were two other people—a baker and a cup bearer for the ruler. Joseph interpreted their dreams, and both those interpretations predicted events which later actually occurred. The baker met with an unfortunate political death. But the cup bearer was returned to his former job, and Joseph begged him to bring his continued imprisonment to the attention of the ruler. The cup bearer promised that he would remember Joseph to the ruler as soon as possible.

The second reader was encouraged by this possible twist of Joseph's story toward a positive end, and she read on with great anticipation.

The setting for the next episode changed from the prison to the ruler's court. Several years had elapsed, and the cupbearer, who had access to the ruler, had forgotten all about Joseph and the promise he had made. However, when the king had a puzzling dream, the cup bearer remembered Joseph and told the ruler of his ability to interpret dreams. The ruler already knew Joseph and had confidence in him because of his previous experience. Joseph was released from prison and interpreted the ruler's dream.

The second reader was overjoyed by this sudden change in Joseph's fate, but when she discovered there was more to the story, she wondered again what the future might hold. . . . Suspense began to build as she continued to allow the story to unfold, not knowing where it might lead.

Joseph was put in charge of the ruler's department of agriculture. Since the interpretation of the dream involved a prediction of many years of plentiful crops, prior to many years of drought, the ruler knew of no one better to plan for the years of drought. Joseph set to work and managed the agricultural system, putting aside food during the years of plenty, so the nation could prepare for the years of drought.

When the years of drought came, the ruler and his people were well prepared because of Joseph's dream interpretation and his administrative and management skills. However, Joseph's father and brothers were not as fortunate. His brothers came for food, but they did not know that it was Joseph they were asking to give them food. Joseph's father was not with the brothers when they came, but Joseph found a way to keep one of his brothers with him while the others were sent home to bring the father. When the father came back with the other brothers, Joseph told them who he was, and there was a glorious reunion.

The first reader's world remained the same, since that person stopped reading about Joseph after the first episode. But the second reader's life was profoundly changed by the story. By following the unfolding plot, the second reader came to realize that difficult circumstances do not always determine the outcome of events. The second reader learned to read life as an unfolding drama, whose outcome one cannot predict until it actually happens. Tragic beginnings don't always have tragic endings.

This story was designed to address the goal—to impact the gloom-and-doom attitude of the counselee. The story was biblical and preplanned to address the attitude through a protocol using two different characters.

## Toward the Twenty-first Century

Storytelling is an art. Some of the clues for this art already exist in African American culture. However, as we continue to be changed by technology, we will need to integrate the natural community traditions with intentional methods, in order to recover and keep alive traditions that will be influenced by technology. Storytelling within African American tradition is alive and well in black churches, yet traditional patterns of care through the use of storytelling are being challenged by such societal influences as the erosion of the extended family.

The major concern for the future is to maintain the indigenous, spontaneous form of caring through stories that exist in the African American tradition. However, we can learn to preserve and enhance this tradition through studying the emerging literature on storytelling. We need to take pride that the academic and professional world of counseling is rediscovering what already was a full-blown tradition in African American culture.

## NOTES

1. For a description of the significance of oral cultures, see Clarence J. Rivers, "The Oral African Tradition Versus the Ocular Tradition," *This Far by Faith: American Black Culture and Its African Roots* (Washington, D.C.: The National Office of Black Catholics, 1977), pp. 38-49.

2. See Philip Barker, *Using Metaphors in Psychotherapy* (New York: Brunner & Mazel, 1985).

3. See Dennis A. Bagarozzi and Stephen A. Anderson, *Personal, Marital, and Family Myths* (New York: W. W. Norton & Co., 1989).

4. See Carol H. Lankton and Stephen R. Lankton, *Tales of Enchantment: Goal-oriented Metaphors for Adults and Children in Therapy* (New York: Brunner & Mazel, 1989).

5. Thomas E. Boomershine, *Story Journeying: An Invitation to the Gospel as Storytelling* (Nashville: Abingdon Press, 1988).

6. Lankton and Lankton, *Tales of Enchantment*, pp. 27-28, 7.

7. For details on the three phases of the counseling process, see Gerard Egan, *The Skilled Helper* (Pacific Grove, Calif.: Brooks Kole, 1990), pp. 28-53.

8. Ibid., p. 71.

# Bibliography

Berinyuu, Abraham. *Pastoral Care to the Sick in Africa: An Approach to Transcultural Pastoral Theology.* Frankfurt: Peter Lang, 1988.

———. *Toward Theory and Practice of Pastoral Counseling in Africa.* Frankfurt: Peter Lang, 1989.

Birchett, Colleen, ed. *How to Help Hurting People.* Chicago: Urban Ministries, Inc., 1990.

Felton, Carroll M., Jr. *The Care of Souls in the Black Church.* New York: Martin Luther King Fellows Press, 1980.

Hollies, Linda H. *Inner Healing for Broken Vessels: Seven Steps to Mending Childhood Wounds.* New York: Welstar Publications, 1990.

Hurst, David. "The Shepherding of Black Christians." Th.D. Dissertation. School of Theology at Claremont, 1981.

Lattimore, Vergel L., III. "The Positive Contribution of Black Values to Pastoral Counseling." *Journal of Pastoral Care* 34 (June 1982): 105-17.

———. "Pastoral Care Strategies of Black Pastors." Ph.D. Dissertation. Northwestern University, 1984.

Mitchell, Henry, and Nicholas C. Lewter. *Soul Theology.* San Francisco: Harper & Row, 1986.

Smith, Archie, Jr. *The Relational Self: Ethics and Therapy from a Black Church Perspective.* Nashville: Abingdon Press, 1982.

Wimberly, Edward P. *Pastoral Care in the Black Church.* Nashville: Abingdon Press, 1979.

———. *Pastoral Counseling and Spiritual Values.* Nashville: Abingdon Press, 1982.

———. *Prayer in Pastoral Counseling.* Louisville: Westminster Press, 1990.

Wimberly, Edward P., and Anne E. Wimberly. *Liberation and Human Wholeness.* Nashville: Abingdon Press, 1986.

# Index